ECONOMIC REFORMS AND REGIONAL IN-EQUALITY IN INDIA

ECONOMIC REFORMS AND REGIONAL IN-EQUALITY IN INDIA

K. GANGADHARAN

SERIALS PUBLICATIONS
NEW DELHI

First Published - 2007

ISBN : 978-81-8387-101-3

The book is published with financial assistance from UGC under its unassigned grant alloted to Kanpur University.

Published by

SERIALS PUBLICATIONS
4830/24, Prahlad Street, Ansari Road
Darya Ganj, New Delhi-110002 (India)
Phone : 23245225 Fax : 91-11-23272135
E-mail: serials@satyam.net.in

Contents

Preface *vii*

About the Editor and Contributors *ix*

PART - I
Introduction

1. Overview 3
– *K. Gangadharan*

PART - II
Health

2. Health Sector and Economic Reforms in India: Some Issues 15
– *K. Ganagadharan*

PART - III
Agriculture

3. Agriculture Growth Assymetries in Kerala-trends and Concerns 33
– *K.P. Mani*

4. Food Security in India: Post-reform Scenario 48
– *N. Radhakrishnan*

PART - IV
Finance and External Sector

5. Post Reform Fiscal Trends in India 67
– *R. Ramachandran*

6. External Sector and Economic Reforms in India 84
—P.S. Mohanakumar

PART - V
Economic Growth, Poverty and Public Distribution System

7. Growth and Inequality in India During the Post Reform Period 95
—K. Rajan

8. Economic Reforms and Regional Disparity 108
—P. Krishna Kumar and C.A. Priyesh

9. Reforms, Growth and Poverty 134
—V.K. Vijayakumar

PART - VI
Tourism

10. Tourism and Information Technology in Kerala A Post Reform Scenario 143
—B. Vijayakumar

PART - VII
Tribal Economy

11. Tribal Economy: Reforms & Unequal Partners 163
—Seetha Kakkoth

12. Economic Reforms and Deprivations of An Artisan Tribe-Kerala Experience 179
—Mini P.V.

Preface

It is about one and a half decade since economic reforms were introduced in India so vigorously in the context of liberalization privatization and globalization. The ultimate goal of economic reforms in India has been the betterment of living conditions of the people especially the deprived and down trodden sections of the society. Hence reforms aimed acceleration of low economic growth of the country which is considered to be the root cause of high incidence of poverty. The new measures have caused varied effects on the economy in general, and also different sectors of the economy in particular. Economists have differences in opinion regarding the impact of economic reforms. The supporters with solid database argue that it has resulted higher economic growth with better standard of living of the people and also reduction in in-equality. The opponents of the reform measures argue that reforms had resulted in large scale unemployment, higher in-equality and poverty and deprivations of the major chunks of the people of India. Though the last 15 years has witnessed rapid economic progress and changes due to new economic policies, studies and research conducted in many parts of the country and different sectors, sections and regions reveals that its benefit are not percolated to all regions, all sectors and all sections of the country equally. There occurred considerable regional, Sectoral, and sectional in-equalities in the distribution of gains of the reforms. This is the context of the present book.

The volume begins with an introduction and the second section deals with a chapter on health sector and economic reforms in India. The third section contains essays on in-equality persisted in the agriculture sector of Kerala and it also deals with the issues connected with the food security in India as part of reform measures.

The fourth section deals with fiscal trends in India as a post reform scenario and also the movement of the external sector of the country during the last 15 years. The fifth section focus on the growth of in-equality and extent of in-equality in growth occurred in different states in India. This section also deals with the problems of poverty, issues connected with the public and the problem of regional disparity occurred in India as a post reform effect. The sixth section emphasis on tourism sector of Kerala and its growth potential in the information technology. The last section examines the tribal economy and it highlight the extent of impact that the economic reforms caused on the tribal folks in Kerala. Since the book is addressed to a wide audience, we have provided data based analytical account of the economic issues and problems. Wherever possible the latest developments have been provided depending on the availability of data. An extensive bibliography at the end of each chapter has also been included for those who wish to use the book as a starting point for further research and study.

This volume is the outcome of the National Seminar conducted by the Department of Applied Economics, Kannur University on 5th and 6th of January 2006. I am grateful to all the 12 scholars who have made significant research contributions to post reform economic issues in India. Special mention may be made of Prof. (Dr.) B.A. Prakash, Head of the Department, Dept. of Economics, University of Kerala, Prof. (Dr.) A.C. Kuttikrishnan, Head of the Department, Dept. of Economics, University of Calicut, Dr. S. Harikumar, Department of Economics, Pondicherry University for their active co-operation and assistance. I am also extremely grateful to the Kannur University for giving the publication grant under the unassigned grant scheme of the UGC for publishing this edited volume. I am deeply indebted to Dr. P. Chandramohan, Vice-Chancellor, Kannur University, Prof. K. Kunhikrishnan, Pro- Vice-Chancellor, Kannur University, Prof. K.M. Abdur Rasheed, Registrar, Kannur University for giving all co-operation and encouragement for bringing the outcome of the National Seminar as an edited volume. I am also grateful to all the colleagues in my department specially Johnson K.A. and V. Shaharban for their active co-operation for to bring this volume.

K. Gangadharan

About the Editor and Contributors

K. Gangadharan is currently Reader and Head, Department of Applied Economics, Kannur University, Kerala. He is the Director of UGC-Population Education Resource Centre of Kannur University and also serving as the Nodal Officer for International Linkage of Kannur University He was formerly Lecturer in the Department of Economics, Pazhassi Raja NSS College, Mattannur in Kerala where he has been teaching since 1994. He has also served as Co-ordinator in the Department of Applied Economics of Kannur University for a short period. Dr. K. Gangadharan has conducted research in the arena of health economics and he has published articles relating to health and social sector issues in leading national and international journals. He has also presented papers in many international and national conferences. Dr. K. Gangadharan has previously written/ published two books titled A Text Book of Banking' in 1999 and 'Utilization of Health Services in Urban Kerala-A Socio-Economic Study' in 2005.

K.P. Mani is Professor, Department of Economics, University of Calicut, Arunattukara, Thrissur. He was formerly the Associate Professor in the College of Co-operation, Banking and Management, Kerala Agricultural University, Thrissur.

N. Radhakrishnan is Selection Grade Lecturer, Post-Graduate Department of Economics, Zamorin's Guruvayoorappan College, Kozhikode, Kerala.

U. Ramachandran is Associate Dean, College of Co-Operation Banking and Management, Kerala Agricultural University, Thrissur, Kerala.

P.S. Mohan Kumar is Selection Grade Lecturer, Post-Graduate Department of Economics, Sree Sankara College, Kalady, Kerala.

K. Rajan is Selection Grade Lecturer, Post-graduate Department of Economics, M.D. College, Pazhanji, Thrissur, Kerala.

P. Krishna Kumar is Selection Grade Lecturer, Post-graduate Department of Economics, Mahatma Gandhi College, Thiruvananthapuram, Kerala.

Priyesh C.A. is Research Scholar in Economics, University of Kerala, Thiruvananthapuram, Kerala.

V.K. Vijayakumar is Selection Grade Lecturer, Department of Economics. Sree Krishna College, Guruvayoor, Kerala.

B.Vijaykumar is Reader in Economics, University College, Thiruvanathapuram.

Seetha Kakkoth is Field Assistant, Department of Anthropology, Kannur University, Thalassery Campus, Palayad.

Mini P.V. is Research Officer, KIRTADS, Kozhikode, Kerala.

PART - I
Introduction

K. GANGADHARAN

1 Overview

The year 1991 marks an important watershed in the economic history of post independent India. The country went through a severe economic crisis triggered by an acute balance of payments situation. The crisis was converted into an opportunity to introduce some fundamental changes in the content and approach to economic policy. The economic reform was initiated with the expectation that many of the economic problems, which had plagued Indian economy would be automatically resolved. For the last 15 years the Indian economy is moving through a very crucial phase. This phase of movement can be put in different versions, some call it as the phase of development and some others as the phase of devaluation of the existing system. Whatever may be the argument the economic reform program started in India resulted in tremendous growth in most of the areas of development. Many of the multy nationalist had come up India and a hike in foreign direct investment also occurred. The markets have been full of products with lot of varieties to meet the consumer's choice. Agriculture had come as big industry with latest technologies and methods. Tourism got boom with many foreigners visiting India. Social sectors also witnessed a drastic improvement in the last one and half decades. But the basic issue is that these benefits are not percolated to all regions, all sectors and all sections of the country equally. There occurred considerable regional and sectoral inequalities in the distribution of the gains of the reforms. This volume focuses on the regional and sectoral inequalities generated in the economy in general and also the inequalities generated in the specific sectors of the economy as part of reform measures. It contains chapters on health sector and economic reforms, economic reforms and public distribution system in India, reforms and agricultural sector of kerala, reforms and food security in India, economic growth and inequality in India, external sector and economic reforms in India, reforms and fiscal crisis, tourism and Infomation technology in Kerala in the eve of reforms, economic reforms and deprivations among tribes, economic reforms and gender inequality, and reforms growth and poverty in India.

The Volume starts with a chapter by K. Gangadharan on health sector and economic reforms in India, examines the impact of economic reforms on the health sector in India and also focus on the issues connected with health sector of kerala as part of the structural adjustment program implemented in India. The study shows the ways in which the structural adjustment program affected the health sector of India and also reveals the underlying forces in the declining role of PHCs in the health care system of India. The paper also shows the increasing health in equalities that persist at the urban rural level in India. It is reflected in the form of the accessibility of heath care institutions, health expenditure, coverage of hospital beds, and availability of doctors, and on paramedical staff. The paper reveals deteriorating quality of public health care institutions, which converts them as mere scarecrows in the field of health delivery system. Since the paper provides thruston the issues of Kerala's health care sector, it reveals the declining of the share of the expenditure on medical and public health in the total development expenditure of the state and also show the proportion of expenditure incurred for medicines of supplies in the total health sector budget of the government of Kerala. The health sector budgets analysis reveals that the expenditure on medicine and supplies has been steadily declining year after years and expenditure on salary and allowance has been on the hike in the last 28 years. The study categorically established that reform program appeared in the dual role of sharp reduction of medical supplies to public health centers on the one side and hike in morbidity of both communicable and chronic illness on the other which converted the life of marginal and vulnerable more horrible and miserable. Paper suggests that effective and solid financial support with proper infrastructural facilities must be provided to the health sector to make it more vibrant and service oriented to meet the health needs of millions of people.

The chapter by K. Rajan on economic growth and inequality in India during the post reform period examines the impact of reforms on economic growth, disparities in economic growth across Indian States and on inequality in India in general. The study examined the growth of Indian economy and growth performance of the states in India during the post reform period in terms of GSDP, per capita GSDP and NSDP etc. Inequality of income or expenditure is measured in terms of percentage of income or expenditure received or spend by the percentage of people in a country. The paper reveals that the economic reforms in India have accelerated economic growth and there are significant differences in the growth states among the Indian states during the post reform period. It also shows that inequality in India get reduced in the post reform period and the trend is towards greater equality.

B. Vijayakumar's chapter on "Tourism and Information technology in Kerala–A post reform scenario" discusses the scope and importance of tourism in Kerala economy and the role of information technology in the development of tourism in the post reform scenario. The author stress on the point of prospects of development of tourism industry in Kerala and its contribution to the development of Kerala economy. The major areas discussed in this section are:

(a) The different policy measures adopted by the Government of Kerala to promote tourism sector in Kerala.

(b) It highlights the consistent growth in the arrival of foreign tourists in Kerala and the phenomenal growth achieved in the tourism earnings.

(c) It focuses on other tourism services since they are the major players of tourism industry.

(d) The paper also highlights the importance of IT sector in the tourism development of kerala.

The chapter by P. Krishna Kumar and C.A. Priyesh discusses the economic reforms and regional disparity with reference to a study conducted on major Indian states on the basis of performance of public distribution system. It starts with the review of the concept of regional disparity. In order to highlight the regional disparities in India the author used some indicators like net state domestic product, percapita income, life expectancy, infant mortality rate, birth rate and death rate and proportion of poor below poverty line. For comparison the authors have selected nine forward states and six backward states. The major conclusions of the study are as follows.

It is found that after the introduction, of reform measures the richer states are becoming more advanced while the backward states are becoming still poorer and backward. In seven out of nine forward states the annual growth rate of percapita income between 1991-2001 is higher than the all India average, where as in all backward states it is found to be much lower than the national average. Infant mortality rate birth rate and death rate are higher in the backward states than the forward states. Along with geographical isolation inadequacy of economic overheads like transport, labour, technology, and lack of access to basic amenities of life and the British rule lead to increase regional disparities in India.

In the second section of the chapter, the authors stressed on the need and importance of PDS in India. They examines the statistical data on consumption of food calorie intake and nutritional outcomes from NSSO, (National Nutrition Monitoring Bureau-NNMB 2001) to justify their stand. They provides the theoretical justification for PDS saying that since inequality of income and wealth exists, purchasing power among the economic agent and marginal rate of substitution for all the people are not equal and PDS helps to correct these to a certain extend. The authors also explains the demand and supply frame work of PDS in the food grain management and establishes that with the help of this system agriculture price can be stabilized. Introduction of reform measures in 1991 has created a major threat to the smooth functioning of PDS in the country and it also changed general structure and pattern of PDS. Through targeted public distribution system has been introduced in the place of PDS, it also subjected to lot of limitations. In the third section the author deals with the performance of PDS in the pre-and post reform period among the major states of India. The performance of PDS in the advanced states in the post reform period shows a positive trend and it is just opposite in the case of backward states in the same period. Thus the author concludes that the reform increased the regional inequality in India and the PDS does .not helps to reduce the regional inequality as expected.

N. Radakrishnan's chapter on food security starts with the discussion of WTO agreements related to agriculture and its impact on Indian agriculture sector. Some structural changes in favour of cash crop is taking place in India and India already entered in the world market for importing rice, one of the important food stuff of Indian people. The author argues that over depends of foreign market for rice will have serious consequences in the future. But in the case of "wheat" the supply is large enough and we need not depend on the world market in the near future. Though India is considered as a food sufficient country, still a large number of people are under starvation because of the inadequate distribution system.

Here the author goes through a broad analysis of the concept of food security and different type of definitions put forward by UNO, World Bank and other agencies and economists. The study arrived at the following conclusions. As the year passes the populations also increases, but the actual production of food grains does not increases as required. The percaipita production of food grains shows a declining trend. The percapita availability of food grain also shows a declining trend. Adequate purchasing power in the hands of people is the most important factor determining food security. Food security should also consider the changing tastes and preferences overcome due to change in the income and standard of living. Scientific management of food stock is a necessary factor of food security. Comparing to 1980's in 1990's the food production and the are a under the production of food has fallen. Though the buffer stock of food grain is more than that of the requirement, its mismanagement and the poor purchasing power of the people lead to starvation and suicides in India.Incresing rural unemployment, decreasing govt. investment in rural development activities, sharp fall in the price of commercial crops and WTO's term lead to fall in the purchasing power of the people.

U. Ramachandran's chapter on post reform fiscal trends in India starts with the discussion of fiscal trends in India starts with the discussion of fiscal condition that existed in the Indian economy during the year 1990-1991. Here he draws out the main causes of fiscal feature during 1990-1991. The author quotes that the new economic policy of India has not diminished the role of state, but it got redefined by expanding it in some area and reducing it in some others. The major conclusions of the discussions are;

(a) The growth trend of gross domestic product of India since 1991 shows a positive trend up to 1994-95 and then it further increased up to 2003-04. But the trend in NSDP of selected few states indicates that almost all states could not achieve the growth rate of 1994-95 in subsequent years.

(b) The combined receipts & disbursement of the central& state Govt shows a declining trend in recent years. Considering the non development and development expenditure of the states most of the state Govts shows that the percentage of non development expenditure is ineveasing.

(c) Considering the deficit indicators of the state Govt. the gross fiscal deficit and revenue deficit shows an increasing trend from 1990-91 to 2003-04 and there after it declined. The primary revenue balance as a percentage of GDP in all post reform period except 2000-01 shows a surplus trend.

(d) The revenue expenditure of the state after the reform period shows an increasing trend.

(e) Expenditure on education, medical & public health also shows an increasing trend in all states after the introduction of reforms.

(f) The debt outstanding of the state shows an increase of more than six fold during 1990-91 and 2004-05, which shows deterioration in fiscal performance and signifies long term mismatch between the growth and revenue expenditure of the state.

(g) The fiscal strength of the economy also affected due to low and declining non-tax revenue, increasing contingent liabilities, poor performance of public sector under taking etc.

K.P. Mani's chapter on agriculture focus on different aspects of Kerala's agriculture performance like irrigation potential, land under cultivation, cropping pattern, subsidies concerned with agriculture, population-growth v/s agriculture growth etc. The author starts with explaining the origin of Kerala State and income trends of the State. The major points of the discussions are as follows:

(a) The State Income and percapita income of Kerala have shown a gradual growth over the years. The development indicators like literacy birthrate, infant mortality, life expectancy etc have also shown a positive trend.

(b) Agriculture is the main occupation of Kerala people which provide employment for 62% of the population and contributes 26% GDP. Reform measures and export oriented growth strategy compelled Kerala to change its cropping pattern towards cash crops.

(c) Though agricultural production has increased as a follow up of green revolution, the agricultural growth and the percapita food grain availability has shown a declining trend.

(d) Uneconomic agricultural operations led to declining trend in the land utilization in kerala and cropping pattern in Kerala. It reveals that there is a sharp decline in the production of rice and area under rice cultivation declined. On the other side the production of cash crops mainly coconut and rubber increased.

(e) The credit availability Kerala farmers from the institutional sources shows a declining trend.

(f) The fertilizer consumption of Kerala agriculture sector shows a sharp increasing trend.

(g) The subsidy till accruing towards agriculture is going up, though the general impression is that all subsidies have been pruned in recent years.

P.S. Mohan Kumar's chapter on "external sector and economic reform" discuss the over all effect of reform interms of various indicators like poverty, unemployment, education, health etc. It starts with the argument that there is a negative linkage between international trade and economic growth in the developing countries. Based on a detailed examination of external sector and growth, the study arrived at the following conclusions;

(a) The external sector during 1990's shows an impressive performance in terms of macro economic indicators like FDI, balance of payment, forex etc.

(b) The FDI related growth depends on strong market and institutional frame work and in the case of developing countries it shows a negative effect.

(c) The correlation between openess and growth are influenced by country specific and locations specific factors. Suitable policies to avert immiserising growth are not effectively taken/implemented in immature economics. This fails to cultivate complementarities between growth and social opportunities.

Seetha Kakoth's chapter on reforms and tribal economy gender perspective examines the gender in equality and gender perspective and the role of gender in the economic activities. The study has been focused on one among the 35 scheduled tribes of kerala viz., the Aranadan, in the context of changed economic situation owing to the commercialization of forest resources, deforestation, non-tribal influx, Acculturation ect. The Aranadan, a dominant tribal community inhabits in the marginal areas of Nilambur forest in Malabar district of kerala and subsist mainly on food gathering, small scale hunting, non

-wood forest produce collection, forest labour and wage labour. The study shows that in the liberalization and globalization along with changes in the immediate ecosystem in the form of plantation activities, deforestation, non tribal influx and acculturation under the folder of economic development of the country, had a negative impact not only on the livelihood pattern of this tribal community, but the entire social institution as well. When the forest were devoid of resources majority of male members within the society resorted to wage labour under non tribes. But females still do their economic pursuits with in the lower valley forest and are least paid or un paid or under paid. When compared to males, women are exposed to the vagaries of cash economy and are exploited by officials, contractors and non tribal immigrants. In short the transition from subsistence economy to market economy resulted in gender bias in access to food within the family and gender in equality in division of labour and payment of wages.

The chapter by Mini P.V. on economic reforms and deprivations of an artisan tribes kerala experience reveals the hard experience felt in the reform era by vettakarumans, one of the artisans tribes of India inhabiting in wynad district of kerala. These tribes were well known for their artistic skill in making hand modelled pottery, weaving gorgeons, baskets and mats They also established their skill in making ploughs and knives like the blacksmith and cut and size the timber like a carpenter. The introduction of reform programmes and huge investment in appliances and machinery in the production of household items and utensils, the traditional craftsmanship of these tribal groups was shattered and they could not sell their products at reasonable prices and they are also starving of markets for these products. The study concluded that their craft forms, requires support, protection, revitalaziation re-vamping and encouragement in the reform era to act as a safety umbrella from the collapse of domestic and foreign competetion faced by the vulnerable sections of Indian society. The study advocates that the reform should increase the productivity of all sections of society by making competition free and access to markets.

V.K. Vijayakumar's chapter on reforms growth and poverty examines the poverty issues with various dimensions of it. He starts with the evaluation of poverty and then provides an overview of world poverty of 1981 and 2001. The paper also explores how economic reforms initiated at the global level affected the growth rate of the economy under different countries and specifically analyzes the poverty problems of India. The study also co-relates poverty and growth, and shows the extent of poverty reduction in India and China for the last 25 years. The paper also provides the need for a strategy to attack poverty and suggests a multipronged strategy to attack poverty.

PART - II
Health

K. GANGADHARAN

Health Sector and Economic Reforms in India: Some Issues

2

INTRODUCTION

Social sector has an indomitant role in the economic advancement of a country. Social sector development consists all those sector which contribute to the enhancement of human capital (Prabhu 1996). Among the social sectors health sector has pivotal role in the economic and social upliftment of a nation.

If we examine certain health care indicators on the eve of economic reforms in India, it can be seen that though India showed remarkable improvement in social sector attainment it fell far short of what had been achieved by other countries in the region. In the case of infant mortality rate, though India showed a decline from a high of 165 in 1960's to 90 in 1991, yet it was high compared to the level of 85 per 1000 live birth recorded by South Korea in 1960. Maternal mortality rate for 1990 was reported at a high of 570 deaths per lakh of female population in India, 370 for Pakistan, 140 for Srilanka and 95 for China. The proportion of underweight infants (0-5 years of age) to its total was also reported at a high of 53 per cent for India in 1987-88, 38 per cent for both Pakistan and Srilanka and 45 per cent for China. Thus on the eve of economic reform measures in 1991 India's achievement in the various components of the health care sector was far below the standard gained by its neighboring nation.

OBJECTIVES OF THE PAPER

The man objectives of the paper are;

1. To examine the impact of economic reforms on the health sector in India.
2. To examine the major issues of health sector in Kerala as part of Structural Adjustment Programme.

STRUCTURAL ADJUSTMENT PROGRAMME & HEALTH SECTOR

The imposition of structural adjustment programme in all the countries culminated in farreaching consequence's for health services development. Today the World Bank and other international bodies are pressing for undoing whatever was built for the national government. State responsibility for the health care is no more considered desirable as it hinders unleashing market forces in the health sector (Quadeer 2001).

The indomitant influence of structural adjustment programme resulted in deteriorating the status and significance of Primary Health Centre in the rural health care delivery system .This culminated in shifting the burden of ill health on to the shoulders of the poor. Epidemics are now being treated not as issues of right to life, but as problems of natural prestige and trade interests, charity and paid voluntarism are being resurrected through foreign funds which ultimately leads to controlling the spheres of investment.

The undue infiuence of structural adjustment resulted in replacing the idea of PHC by WHO's new public health (WHO 1996). It involves and underlines the following package of services.

1. Abolition of the notion of planning for population as a natural agenda and talks of healthy cities and communities, thereby shifting responsibility to the local organization.
2. Within NPH (new public health) the role of state becomes so insignificant that it is forced to seek partners in the private corporate and NGO sectors.
3. The PHC approach emphasizes adequately and equally distributed health resources and social measures, whereas the NPH only concerns itself with health status.

4. From essential health care for the main health problems, it moves on to "prevention of the preventable".
5. Despite these shifts it claims, socio-economic growth is its anchor, where in priorities have to be set between treatment of disease and affecting its determinants. However since it accepts "the finiteness" of resources and the logic of cutbacks in the social sector and also hazardous and iniquitous growth of the economy, its only recourse is in encouraging individuals to take action and make practical work plan to save themselves from increasing risks. It does not question the risk themselves.
6. It claims operational freedom from the subordination of medicine.
7. At the same time it states that, the greatest insights into determinants of health are held by the staff of health facilities and hospitals. Thus while it reduces disease control activities in health sector, it retains the emphasis on the theraputics.
8. It focuses on the special needs of individuals through their life cycles. Interestingly, the emphasis of the life cycle approach is on the reproductive phase of the life of woman. While the market is allowed to occupy the empty spaces created by a receding public sector in health, the latter influenced by the truncated vision of life cycle depends entirely on reproductive health strategy to control fertility.
9. Technology based disease control programme replace social strategy based programs of public distribution systems of food and drinking water.

The structural adjustment programmes involve stringent measures for regulating the drain of resources of the public sector. It includes (Werner etal 1996):

(a) Sharp cuts in public spending on health, education and other social services.

(b) The removal of subsidies and lifting of price controls on staple foods and other basic commodities.

(c) Freezing of wages.

(d) A shift from production of food and goods for domestic consumption to production for export.

(e) Liberalization of trade policies.

(f) Privatization of public services and state enterprises, and

(g) Devaluation of local currency.

The Indian economy witnessed vital macro economic and structural changes in 1990. The hard cakes of deregulation privatization and integration with global economy were also tasted by the health sector in a country like India with large proportion of the population below the official poverty line where caste still correlate with economic well being especially for the poorest in rural areas and with a long history of gender in equality the extent to which health services are equitable plays a crucial role in the well being and indeed survival of those who are disadvantaged (Gitasen etc). Though the Bhore committee (Govt. of India 1946) highlighted the inequality eroded in the health sector even after five decades of planned development in equalities in the health care sector in India is still a vital issue and the failures of the system have driven both the rich and poor towards private health providers.

Despite the best efforts the status of health in India has been a victim of widening disparities. The disparities in the health sector varies from number of institution operating in the rural and urban areas, number of doctors and paramedical person working in the rural and urban regions, availabilities of essential drugs and medicine working in the rural and urban regions availabilities of essential drugs and medicine.

The major health indicators of selected countries along with India (table 1) revealed that India was lagging behind the selected countries except Pakistan in life expectancy at birth and infant mortality. Only 28% of people in India had access to improved sanitation facilities, while it was 100 per cent in Singapore, 94 per cent in Srilanka and so on. India was much behind Pakistan, Bangladesh and Singapore in the percentage of population having access to water resources.

The total health expenditure as a percentage of GDP was estimated as 4.9% for the period 1997. 2000 (World

Development Indicators 2003) in India was less compared to 5.3% in China.

Table 1
Health Indicators in Selected Countries

Countries	*Life expectancy at birth*	*IMR per 1000 life birth*	*Access to improved water source % of population*	*Access to improved sanitation facility (%)*
India	63	67	84	28
China	70	31	75	38
Pakistan	63	84	90	62
Bangladesh	62	51	97	48
Singapore	78	3	100	100
Sri Lanka	73	17	77	94

Source: World Development Indicators 2003.

There is need to enhance the outlay for health, ensure the equitable distributing between status, narrow the urban rural gap and remove the lacunae impeding effective delivery of health care services at the community level both in rural and urban areas, where a sizable population live in slums which has no access to affordable health care despite proliferation of private practitioners, nursing homes and corporate hospitals.

HEALTH IN EQUALITIES AT THE RURAL URBAN LEVEL

Accessibility of health care facilities in India at the rural and urban level is highly un-equal in nature. Urban areas and economically advanced regions attract a larger share of health resources than needed by their share in the total population whereas economically backward and remote area remains constantly under served. In 1991, only 32% of all hospitals, 20% of hospital beds and no more than an estimated 41% of all trained doctors were in rural areas, where over 70% of the population still lives (Duggal etal 1995).

Rural areas received a declining share of qualified practitioners between 1961 and 1981, even as medical education in the country expanded, mainly in private colleges recognized by different medical councels (Jesani with Anantharaman 1993). In Ahmednagar District of Maharashtra State, even in rural areas average population to doctor ratio, were 812:1 and 1806:1 in developed and under-developed taluks (sub-division of the district) respectively (Sule 1999).

DETERIORATING QUALITY AND DECLINING SHARE OF PUBLIC HEALTH SERVICES

The share of health in the Government's revenue expenditure (both Centre and State together), which was 2.7% in 1950-51, peaked at 5.1% in 1960-61 and then began to decline. The decline was particularly evident in the first half of the 1990's by 1994-95, it had in fact fallen to 2.6% (Duggal etal. 1995).

The referral hospitals functioning in most part of the countries is poorly equipped to cater the needs of the people. The major problem faced by the CHC's and PHC's in the country is that qualified and experienced hands are unwilling to associate with these institutions. The striking facts in this regard can be noticed in the case of Uttar Pradesh, where 82% of the sanctioned posts of Gynecologists and Obstetricians were vacant in the year 1992. Similarly at the end of March 1993, some 68% of all posts earmarked for Pediatricians, in Gujarat were also vacant. (Central Bureau of Health Intelligence 1994). These insufficiencies and inefficiencies culminated in acute shortages in even the most essential drugs and equipment in public health institutions in rural areas (Phadke etal. 1995).

Though 1991 is treated as the year in which India launched reform measures, the available data and investments in the health sector clearly revealed that, the Indian health sector began to move in the deregulation and liberalization path in the 1980's itself.

The declining share of public hospital and dispensaries in public health expenditures since the 1980's coincided with a growing number of private hospitals that received state support through public financial assistance and tax exemptions. This type of public subsidy to the private sector further skewed the urban bias in health resources. Private health services tend to be clustered around places that are better provisioned with public health facilities and infrastructure. This is usually in urban or more economically advanced areas.

The study made by Rane (Rane 1996) clearly reveals the impact of liberalizations on the pharmaceutical industry in India. Between 1980 and 1995 there occurred a 197% overall hike in the cost of drugs (i.e. around 778 drugs surveyed for the study). The sharpest increases averaging 336% were evident for anti-cancer drugs, many of which are imported, and also for those drugs that have a near monopoly. Several drugs that have to be taken over long periods of time, such as those for thyroid disorders, had increased over 500%. The prices of inessential drugs and irrational combinations such as balms, anti-diarroheals, antiobesity drugs, laxatives, enzymes, food products and some nutritional activities also increased.

HEALTH CARE COSTS

The major cost involved in the health care of people are medical fees, costs of drugs, diagnostic facilities, institutional care and travel costs to the facility. In addition to this the opportunity cost in terms of wages lost not only of the patient but also of the bystanders/supporters for inpatient/outpatient case respectively must also be taken into account.

Compared with the mid 1980's costs of both outpatient and inpatient care rose in rural and urban areas. The table 2 reveals that between 1986-87 and 1995-96, in rural areas, private outpatient cost went up by 142% at against 77% in the public sector. In urban areas, private outpatient costs increased by 150% compared with 124% in the public sector. The urban rural price difference for outpatient care also shows an increasing trend over 1986-87 to 1995-96. In the case of inpatient care also the trends revealed a hike in the costs over 1986 to 1996. It mounts to 436% in rural and 320% in urban areas. The N.S.S. organization data for 1998 revealed that hospitalization costs to the poor in government hospitals appeared to be significantly higher in 1995-96 than in other hospitals in the rural areas. The average total expenditure per hospitalization in the so called free wards of government hospitals is more than 20% higher in other hospitals.

District surveys in Maharastra and Madhya Pradesh during the late 1980's and early 1990's and the study conducted in

Kerala by the Kerala Sastra Sahithya Parishad in 2005 showed that expenditure on health as a proportion of total household consumption expenditure was higher among groups belonging to lower socio economic classes (Duggal with Amin 1989, George etal 1997).

Table 2
Average Expenditure on Medical Care in India, 1995-96

	Rural 1995-96	*Change %* 1986-96	*Urban* 1995-96	*Change%* 1986-96	*Urban rural ratio* 1986-96
Outpatient care					
Public sector	129	77	166	124	1.2
Private sector	186	142	200	150	1.08
Totals	176	132	194	146	1.10
Inpatient care					
Public sector	2080	549	2195	470	1.06
Private sector	4300	486	5344	343	1.24
Totals	3202	436	3921	320	1.22

Source: National Sample Survey Organization 1998.

The hike in health care costs across the country revealed that it had adversely affected the deprived and down trodden groups in the society which further resulted in increasing their indebtedness gender and age biases in health seeking behavior and also growing volume of untreated morbidity (National Sample Survey Organization 1998).

The gravity of untreated morbidity can be realized, if we examine the reasons for no treatment illness of in the case of person ailing from different illness. The table 3 shows the reasons for no treatment in India during the period 1986-87 and also in 1995-96.

The table reveals that the percentage of people who were alienated from the health services utilization due to financial stringency went up significantly in both rural and urban areas. At the same time all of them began to provide due services for their illness and the percentage of people who did not consider their illness not serious has steadily diminished over the period.

It is hypothesized that financial reasons had played an indomitant role in the generation of health care in equalities in India especially after the reform era. The class based inequalities in access to health services has really sharpened for both men and women and poor households are beyond the ambit of accessibility and affordability of health care services (National Sample Survey Organization 1992).

Table 3
Reason for No Treatment in India-1986-1996

Reason for no treatment	Rural %		Urban %	
	1986-87	1995-96	1986-87	1995-96
No Medical facility	3	9	0	1
No faith in medicine	2	4	2	5
Long waiting	0	1	1	1
Financial stringency	15	24	10	21
Illness not serious	75	52	81	60
Other reasons	5	10	6	12
Total	100	100	100	100

Source: National Sample Survey Organization 1998.

STRUCTURAL ADJUSTMENT PROGRAMME AND KERALA EXPERIENCE

To measure the actual impact of structural Adjustment programme, it is necessary to examine the health profile of Kerala. Although the health status of Kerala has been praised world over recent report suggest that it stands on a week base (Ekbal and Raman Kutty 1996). The report reveals that pacific health system in the state has collapsed and the government hospitals have lost their credibility. This ultimately culminated in declining investment in the health sector and entry of private sector into the health care sector. About 60%of hospitals and health workers including doctors are in the private sector which is accessible to 30-40% of the people (Nayar 1998).

Table 4 reveals the major health status indicators in the state in comparison to all India's figure.

Though the health services of the State Govt. has an important role for this achievement measures taken in the last one decades reveals that the significance of Govt sector in the health care of the state has diminished greatly. The relevant data on health care investment shows that Govt. was responsible for the deteriorating role of public sector in the health care sector of kerala. Since part of the health programs of the states are financed by Central Govt. funding the expenditure compression initiated as part of structural adjustment programme by the Govt. of India affected the Govt. of Kerala too in their health care expenditure.

Table 4
Constant Birth Rate, Death Rate, Infant Mortality Rate and Maternal Mortality Rate in India and Kerala-2004

Indicators	*Kerala*	*India*
Birth rate (per 1000 population)	16.90	25.00
Death rate (per 1000 population)	6.40	8.10
IMR (per 1000 live birth)	10.00	63.00
MMR (per 1000 population)	0.87	4.37
Life expectancy Male	70.00	64.10
Female	73.62	65.60

Economic review-2005.

TRENDS IN DEVELOPMENT EXPENDITURE ON HEALTH AND FISCAL CRISIS IN KERALA

The table 4 shows trends in development expenditure and it highlights the proportion of expenditure incurred on medical, public health and family planning. Expenditure on medical, publc health as a proportion of total development expenditure shows steady decline in the 1990's. It was 16.4% in 1989-1990 and reached to 12.2% 2000-2001.

It reveals that the decline in public investment as a package of reform measures adversely affected the health sector of Kerala public health care institutions in India increasingly face the problem of resource stringency ever since the era of reform measures. The paradox is that this is happening at a time when the cost of health care is increasing at a rate higher than the index of general commodities due to the application of more expensive technologies to medical care. The financial crisis occurred in Kerala was very severe in the end of 1990's and that the Govt. was unable to clear huge arrears of payments to suppliers of medicine and consumable for hospitals. (Govt. of Kerala 2001).

Table 5
Trends in Development Expenditure (Revenue)
(Amount Rs in lakhs)

Year	*Total Development expenditure*	*Expenditure on Medical public health and Family Planning*	*III as % of II*
I	*II*	*III*	*IV*
1986-87	111520	14345	12.8
1987-88	116293	16653	14.9
1988-89	135888	21420	15.7
1989-90	146031	23956	16.4
1990-91	180260	27850	15.4
1991-92	196912	29200	14.8
1992-93	228060	30130	13.2
1993-94	258597	36744	14.2
1994-95	301538	43157	14.3
1995-96	341216	49862	14.6
1996-97	404796	53533	13.2
1997-98	503126	63412	12.6
1998-99	564203	69486	12.3
1999-2000	665420	90329	13.5
2000-01	717048	87822	12.2

Source: Economic Review 2003.

Poor performance of the public health sector really affects the deprived sections in the rural and urban areas who are the main stakeholders of the public sector health care services. The opening up of the health sector to the private sector facilitates access to higher levels of health care services by the better of, but neglects the poor for e.g., access to innovation such as tele medicine is restricted to the educated and rich sections of the populations.

The result is the medical poverty trap with more and more people likely to remain untreated. This conflicts with principle of universal coverage of health care and shared risk upheld by the tax funded health system (Price *et al.*, 1999).

Recently the Governments are forced by International institutions to withdraw from investing in public goods or in the so called soft sectors. In areas like Alleppy in Kerala, which were producing food crops for local consumption, there is tremendous pressure on food security system because of export orientation and extensive cash crop cultivation withdrawal of subsides and credit facilities as part of structural adjustment programs have farther affected the food production levels and therefore nutritional standards of households in the regions have suffered. (Sebastian 2001).

Table 6
Morbidity due to major Communicable illness in Kerala in 1994 and 2004

Diseases	*1995*		*2004*	
	Attack	*Death*	*Attack*	*Death*
Acute diarrhoeal disease	700974	16	541438	17
Whooping cough	1566	-	198	-
Measles	7026	1	4942	1
Chicken pox	-	-	14920	8
Acute Respiratory infection	31,89,579	130	81,31,103	216
Pneumonia	18955	28	29475	59
Enteric fever	8413	6	12996	3
Viral Hepatitis A	10489	11	7433	11
Viral Hepatitis B	-	-	2162	97
Rabies	149	9	31	-
Pulmonary tuberculosis	39241	278	20836	187
All other diseases	1,11,65,090	4336	2,32,58,663	7889
Total	1,51,41,482	4815	3,20,24,825	8528

Source: Directorate of Health Services, Thiruvananthapuram.

Another important factor which affects the health care sector of Kerala in recent years is the hike in morbidity. Table 5 provides morbidity due to major communicable illness in Kerala in 2004. The morbidity prevalence of communicable illness in Kerala for the last nine years increased to an extent of 154.92% in the case of acute respiratory infection, 55.49% in the case of pneumonia, 54.47% in the case of enteric fever, and 108.3% in the case of all other diseases. The overall prevalence of communicable illness increased to 115.5% for the last 9 years.

What is more shocking in the Kerala health care system is that on the one side morbidity of both communicable and non communicable diseases is increasing on the one side and the proportion of amount allocated for medicines and supplies in the government health budget is steadily declining on the other. (Gangadharan 2005) The hike in morbidity of communicable illness is mainly due to lack of proper drinking water, sanitation, drainage, proper housing facilities etc. (see table 1 to examine the status of Indian with sanitation and drinking water supplies). The chronic illness is also increasing due to the change in life style of the people, influence of the foreign investment in consumer items, worsening of the environment due to the operation of the multinational corporations in the chemical engineering, mining, cement, and other environmental disastrous industries. Table 7 shows the proportion of allocation under health budget of Government of Kerala from 1980 to 2003.

Table 7
Budget Allocation for Different Expenditure Head of the Health Department (in percentage)

Expenditure Item	*Period*			
	1980	*1990*	*1995*	*2003*
Pay allowances	52.24	62.48	66.46	69.31
Office expenses	4.34	3.35	3.74	1.01
Medicines	31.16	25.43	23.09	16.14
Hospital accessories	4.91	2.36	2.07	3.04
Vehicles	0.22	0.21	0.11	0.66
Construction	5.18	2.85	2.77	3.94
Grants-in-aid	1.96	3.33	1.76	5.90

Source: Budget documents, Government of Kerala, various years.

From the table 6, it can be seen that pay and allowances as an expenditure Item recorded a rapid jerk of 52% in 1980 to around 70% in 2003. At the same time the of expenditure offered to medicines and supplies steadily declined to an extent of about 50% over the same period. The high level of political consciousness in the state, strong unions and previously balanced governments, together created a political environment in which curtailment of salary expense was not easy. On the other hand the curve for supplies shows a much gentler upward slope all throughout the eighties indicating a moderate degree of increase. Successive Governments faced with the necessity of controlling revenue expenditure but denied the choice of ever trying to check the growth of salaries were left with no option but to reduce spending on supplies, which ultimately denied the basic health services to the poor.

CONCLUSION

The economic reforms initiated in India from 1991 onwards adversely affected in the delivery of the minimum required health services for the deprived and vulnerable section of the Indian community. The rapid reduction in Government allotment to health care sector and mass reduction in public health care investment converted the rural and urban health centers as mere scare scrow. Though the economic reform programs resulted in the massive private investment which culminated in proliferation of private practitioners, nursing homes and corporate hospitals, they are unaffordable and inaccessible for the poor communities in the rural and urban areas and also those who live in slums. The economic reforms also engineered the expansion of the commercial crops to capture the global market and reduction in food crops on the one side, and the withdrawal of food subsidy resulted a sharp reduction in food production level and also sharp decline in the nutritional standards of the people in the country.

The reform programme in the health sector in India has been pursuing as an unfinished agenda. It appeared in the dual role of sharp reduction of medicinal supplies to public health centers on the one side and a hike in morbidity of both communicable and chronic illness on the other which converted the life of the marginals and vulnerable more horrible and miserable .Effective and solid financial support with proper infrastructural aid must be provided to the health sector to make it more vibrant and service oriented to meet the health needs of the millions of people.

REFERENCES

Gita Sen, Asha George and Asha George (2002), Class Gender and Health Equity, Lessons from Liberalizing India in Engendering International Health ed. by Gita Sen, Asha Georoge and Prosler Ostling, The M 11 Press, London.

Govt. of India (1946), Report of the Health Survey and Development Committee Vols. 1-4 (Bhore Committee), Superintendent of Govt. Printing, New Delhi.

Sule M. (1999), Health Manpower in the District in Health Resources, Investment and Expenditure–A Study of Health Providers in a District in India.

Rane W. (1996), Analysis of Drug Prices, 1980-95 EPW August 24-31.

Duggal R. and Amin S. (1989), Cost of Health Care. A Household Survey in an Indian District, Bombay, Foundation for Research in Community Health.

George, A. Shah I. and Nandaraj S. (1997), Morbidity, Health Care Utilization and Expenditure Madhya Pradesh 1990-91. In Household Health Expenditure in Two States. Comparative Study of Districts in Maharashtra and Madhya Pradesh, Pune/ Mumbai, Foundation for Research in Community Health.

National Sample Survey Organization (1992), Morbidity and Utilization of Medical Services (NSS 42nd Round 1986-87) Sarvekshana 52 (XV).

National Sample Survey Organization (1998), Morbidity and Treatment of Ailments. Report 441, NSS Fifty Second Sound, July 1995–June 1996, New Delhi: Dept. of Statistics, Govt. of India.

World Bank (1998), World Developement Indicators by Washington DC, World Bank.

World Bank (2003), World Development Indications, Washington DC: World Bank.

Central Bureau of Health Intelligence (1994), Health Information of India New Delhi, Govt. of India.

Phadke, A., Fernandez A., Sharda L. and A. Jessani (1995), A Study of Drug Supply and use of Pharmaceuticals in Satara District, Mumbai, Foundation for Resources in Community Health.

Liu, U.L., Hsino, W.C. LIQ, Liu X.Z. and M.H. Rew (1995), Transformation of China's Rural Health Care Financing, Social Science and Medicine LI (8) 1085-1093.

Makinen, M., Waters H., Rauch M., Almagam betvou N., Bitran R., Gilson, L. Metntyre, Pannaranothai S., Prieto A.L., Ubilla G., In-Equalities in Health Care use and Expenditure. Empirical Data from Eight Developing Countries or Countries in Transition Bulletin of W.H.O. 78 (1): 55-65.

Ekbal, B. and Ramankutty K. (1996), Health Handbook for Workers, Trivandrum, Kerala Sastra Sahitya Parishad.

Nayar, K.R. (1998), Old Priorities and New Agenda of Public Health in India. Is there a mismatch? Croation Medical Journal 39(3): 308-315.

Sebastian K.S. (2001), Public Health Issues of small Towns: The Case of Allepy in Public Health and the Poverty of Reforms, The South Asian Predicament edhy Quadeer Imrana, Sen Kasturi and Nayar K.R. New Delhi, Sage Publications.

Werner, D., Snders D., Weston J., Babb S. and Rodriguez B. (1996), Questioning the Solution: The Politics of Primary Health Care and Child Survival Palo Alto: Health Wrights.

WHO (1996), New Challenges for Public Health. Report of Inter Regional Meetings, Nos. 27-30, 1995. Geneva: WHO Quader Imrana (2001). Impact of Structural Adjustment Programmes and concepts in Public Health, in Public Health and Poverty of Reforms and by Imrana Qader, Kasturi Sen and K.K. Nayar, New Delhi. Sage Publications.

Gangadharan, K. (2005), Utilization of Health Services in Urban Kerala, a Socio-Economic Study, New Delhi, Serials Publications.

Government of Kerala (2001), White paper: State Finances, Thiruvanandapuram: Govt. of Kerala.

Seetha Prabhu, K. (1996), Social Sectors in Economic Development. Some Issues, Conference Volume.

Jugale, V.B. (2005) World Trade Organizations and India, Econimic Reforms, New Delhi, Serials Publications.

Duggal, R. Nandaraj S. and A. Vadair (1995), Health Expenditure Across States Part I, Economic and Political Weekly April 15.

Jesani, A. and Anandaraman S. (1993), Private Sector and Privatization in the Health Care Service, a review paper for the ICSSR-ICMR Joint panel on Health.

PART - III
Agriculture

K.P. Mani

Agriculture Growth Assymetries in Kerala-trends and Concerns

3

When India became free, three administrations ruled this region–two princiley states, Travancore and Cochin, and Malabar which was under the direct admistration of the British. One of the first steps taken by independent India was to amalgamate small states together so as to make them viable administrative units. Accordingly, Travancore and Cochin states were integrated to form the Travancore Cochin state on Ist July, 1949. However, Malabar remained as part of the Madras province. Under the state Reorganzation Act of 1956, Travancore Cochin states and Malabar were united to form of the state of Kerala on Ist November, 1956. The state represents only 1.18 per cent of the total area of india but 3.43 per cent of the total population of the country is in Kerala.

From table I it is evident that the state income has made gradual growth over the years. The state income in current prices made 49.84 times increase over 1950 and 1999. During the same period, per capita income at current prices made only in increace of 32.76 times. Further between 1990-91 and 2003-2004, state per capita income at current prices increased by 5.86 and 5.23 times respectively. These trends indicate that disproportionate population size compared to the share of the state in the total country area are root causes of her many problems like low per capita income and huge unemployment. The sreverity of the problem of low per capita income will be crystal clear when we realize that the state is ranked 15th (2003) in terms of per capita income among the 28 states in india.

Table 1
State Income Profile

Year	*State (current price) (Rs. crore)*	*State income (1980-81 prices) (Rs. crore)*	*Per capita income (current prices)*	*Per capita income (1980-81 price)*
1970-71	1255	1255	594	594
1980-81	3823	3823	1508	1508
1990-91	10668	4892	3718	1705
1994-95	28375	25335	9327	8327
1999-00	62557	27319	1946	8617
2004-05*	89451	44054	27048	13321

Source: Govt. of Kerala Economic Review. *refers to quick estimates and the base is 1993-94.

The Kerala state, despite its low per capita income, displays a set of unusually high development indicators such as adult literacy, life expectancy, infant mortality and birth rate. The Kerala model, especially the performance of its quality of life indicators has attracted wide spread attention. The state enjoys a high percentage of literacy equal to that in the USA. According to the 1991 census, adult and female literacy are 94.45 per cent and 86.93 per cent respectively, compared to the All India figures of 63.86 per cent and 39.42 per cent. Life expectancy also stood above the All India level. Male life expectancy rate increased from 68 years in 1991 to 72 years in 2001 from 46 in 1961, while female life expectancy improved from 50 years in 1961 to 56 in 2001. The improvement in health care is further reflected in the favourable infant mortality rate and birth rate. Infant mortality rate improved from 120 in 1961 to 22 in 1991 and 13 in 2001 (See table 2).

Various hypotheses have been formulated for the conflicts in Kerala's development experience which can be sum up in the dual issues of low per capita income and high performance in human development indicators. One hypothesis, which is traditional, is the backwardness in agriculture and industry sectors.

Table 2
Trends in Development Indicators

	India 1961	*Kerala 1961*	*India 1971*	*Kerala 1971*	*India 1981*	*Kerala 1981*	*India 1991*	*Kerala 1991*	*India 2001*	*Kerala 2001*
Literacy										
a) males	34	54	40	54	47	75	63	94	75.85	94.20
b) females	13	38	19	66	25	65	39	86	54.16	87.86
Birth rate (1000)	42	39	41	37	37	26	31	17	24.80	16.70
Infant mortality (1000)	165	120	129	61	114	39	58	22	60	11
Life expectancy (years)	42	46	46	61	57	65	59	68	65.10	73.67
Males	41	50	45	62	50	63		68	64.10	71.67
Females	44	52	49	64	51	67		71	65.80	75.00

Source: Government of Kerala Economic Review.

PRELUDE

Conventional economics believed that the agriculture sector is the back bone of the Indian economy. To a great extent, this argument is valid also because even after significant structural changes in the Indian economy as a consequence of reforms, the sector contributes nearly 26 per cent of Gross Domestic Product, provides employment for 62 per cent of the population and liberally contributes towards foreign exchange earnings (2004). These reforms process and the resultant changes brought some rapid tilts in the behaviour and performance of the agricultural sector. One important consequence is the notable shifts in cropping pattern skewed in favour of cash crops. These trends are the result of two factors. Firstly, the shift in cropping pattern is a trend started by late 1980 at the national level and various reasons can be attributed for this. Secondly, reforms process compelled this shift because of the new strategy of export led growth. The cropping pattern in favour of cash crops necessitated substantial changes in the composition of inputs and also its distribution. In this context it is appropriate to examine the growth trends since reforms and examine its pattern and distribution.

AGRICULTURE GROWTH MACRO PERSPECTIVES

The mid sixties which were marked by the beginning of the green revolution was something like a watershed in the growth of the Indian agriculture. During the pre revolution period, production of all crops recorded an impressive average growth rate of 3.13 per cent per annum. During the subsequent period, the growth rate remained subdued at 2.10 per cent. The rate of expansion of agricultural production was remarkably higher during the eighties. The production indices of food grains showed a steep rising trend through out the decade except for a downward movement during 1986-87 and 1987-88. More spectacular was the rising trend in the output of non food grains particularly during the second half of the decade. The production of all crops recorded a growth rate of 2.77 per cent during the first half of the eighties, and it accelerated to 3.92 per cent during the second half of the decade, compared with 2.10 per cent during 1964-65. During the nineties, however the growth rate of agricultural production slowed down considerably to 2.64 per cent and the growth rate of food grains decelerated to 1.63 per cent. Not only that the growth rate decelerated, the absolute production levels of food grains remained far below the plan targets also. Food grains output failed to keep pace with the population growth and consequently, the per capita availability of food grains which had reached a level of 510 grams per day in 1991 declined to an average level of 482 gram per day during the subsequent years and reached 464 gram per day in 2002. These broad trends in the growth rates of agricultural production are directly or indirectly linked to a series of related issues like input supply, markets, price policy, trade policy etc.

Table 3 clearly established that the growth rate in area under different crops is not capable of compensating the changes in the population growth. On the other hand reasonable increase is reported in the yield factor which is the direct consequence of technology, but that change has mainly taken place only in the non food crops. These trends are very evident in Kerala state also. One may apriori feel that the change is reasonable and in tune with the current strategy of export led growth. But a disproportionate growth in non food crops with out adequate support and linkages retard the agricultural growth of the state which will be clear from the forthcoming discussions.

Table 3
Population Growth v/s Agricultural Growth (%)

Year	*total population million*	*annulal growth of population*	*period*	*area%*	*yield%*	*production %*
1951	361.1	1.25	1949/50 1964/65	1.61	1.50	3.13
1961	439.2	1.96	1967/68 1980/81	0.54	1.82	2.38
1971	548.2	2.20	1980/81 1990/91	0.05	3.16	3.21
1981	685.2	2.22	1949/50 1991/92	0.64	2.05	2.70
1991	844.3	2.11	1959/60 1999/00	0.87	2.87	1.96
2001	1040	1.98	1969/70 2000/01	0.97	2.97	1.54
			1979/80 2000/01	1.04	2.58	1.79
			1989/90 2000/01	1.64	2.97	1.57
			1999/00 2000/01	1.96	2.99	1.84
			2001/02	2.04	2.64	1.91

Source: Agricultural statistics at a glance, Government of India, New Delhi 2004.

TRENDS IN LAND UTILIZATION IN KERALA

Any discussion on agricultural sector starts with examining the land utilization pattern and the profile of land holdings which are available from tables 4. From table 4 it is seen that since 1990, the gross cropped area made a notable decline from 302000 hectors to 2271000 hectors the rate of fall being 24.80 per cent. This is mainly due to the shifts of the farmers from agricultural operations to non agricultural operations mainly arguing that the agricultural operations are becoming uneconomic because of escalating input prices and increasing labour cost. Another notable feature is the significant shift in cropping pattern skewed towards cash crops.

Table 4
Trends in land utilization Kerala ('00 hector)

	1975-76	*1980-81*	*1985-86*	*1990-91*	*1995-96*	*1997-98*	*2004-05*
Total geographical area	38855	38855	38855	38855	38855	38855	38855
Forest	10815	10815	10815	10815	10815	10815	10815
Net sown area	21892	21796	21910	22468	22690	22860	21727
Total cropped area	29813	28848	28666	30200	30660	22710	29424

Source: Economic Review Government of Kerala.

TRENDS AND GROWTH PATTERNS IN AREA UNDER VARIOUS CROPS

Table 5 provides a clear picture and trends of the cropping pattern in the state from 1960-61 to 2000. Out of the gross cropped area of 2349 thousand hectares in 1960-61, rice occupied 778.91 hectares, forming 33.15 per cent of the gross cropped area. But the share of gross cropped area under rice consistently came down to 28 per cent in 1980-81 and 15.45 per cent in 2000, and absolute terms, the area under rice declined to 678.28 thousand hectares in 1980-81, the average annual fall being 0.68 per cent. Further between 1980-81 and 2000, the area under rice declined by 30.53 per cent, absolute fall during the 15 years period being 207.13 thousand hectares. The fall in cumulative area in 1995-96, compared to 1960-61 being 307.76 thousand hectares. The area divided for all food crops together was about 46 per cent in 1960-61 but it came down to just 16.52 per cent in 1999-00. The important reasons being the domination of cash crops like coconut and rubber which is evident from further examination. In the year 1960-61, coconut constituted 21.31 per cent and rubber constituted 5.23 per cent of the gross cropped area. These shares marginally improved to 22.77 per cent and 8.24 per cent respectively by 1980-81. But since 1980-81, there is a tremendous leap. The area under coconut reached 982.10 thousand hectares in 1995-96, almost double the area in 1990-91. Similarly, area under rubber reached 449.00 thousand hectares in 1995-96, an increase of 3.68 times compared to 1960-67. While the area under rice declined by 336.55 thousand hectares between 1980-81 and 2000-01, area under coconut and rubber increased by 330.73 thousand and 211.23 thousand hectares during the same period. These three crops constituted 60 per cent of the gross cropped in 1960-61 and 62 per cent in 2000 and the trends clearly establish the claim that Kerala farmers are shifting the area under rice to coconut and rubber while the state is 50 per cent short in rice production compared to consumption requirements and when the state lacks linkages to absorb coconut an d rubber.

Table 5
Gross Cropped area under major Crops in Kerala
(1960-61-1999-2005 000ha)

2	*Crops*	*1960-61*	*1970-71*	*1980-81*	*1985-86*	*1990-91*	*1999-00*	*2004-05*
1.	Rice	778.91	874.93	NA	NA	559.45	348.20	289.97
		(61.20)	(57.67)			(52.40)	(50.34)	(49.62)
2.	Coconut	500.76	719.14	651.37	704.68	870.02	1080.0	897.76
		(56.64)	(56.96)	(47.61)	(43.31)	(45.02)	(62.83)	(54.61)
3.	Rubber	122.87	179.26	237.77	330.32	384.00	469.9	480.54
		(13.90)	(14.18)	(17.36)	(20.30)	(19.95)	(28.72)	(29.46)
4.	Coffee	16.80	31.56	57.95	65.64	75.05	83.7	84.64
5.	Tea	37.63	37.59	36.16	34.74	34.71	36.8	NA
6.	Other Plantations	205.91	295.90	385.88	491.35	560.35	NA	NA

Figures in brackets corresponding to rice indicates the share of the area of rice in the total area under food crops and for other crops the figures in brackets indicate the percentage share to area under non food crops.

Source: Compiled from:

1. Government of Kerala (1975), Agricultural Statistics in Kerala, The Bureau of Economics and statistics, Thiruvananthapuram.
2. Government of Kerala, Economic Review (for various years) State Planning Board, Thiruvananthapuram.
3. CMIE (1999) India's Agricultural Sector - A Compendium of Statistics Bombay, July.

In the succeeding section an attempt is made to examine the inter district, intra district and inter temporal shifts in cropping pattern with reference to rice, coconut and rubber on production and yield.

CROPPING PATTERN INTER DISTRICT ANALYSIS

Table 6
Gross Change in Area Between 1975-76 & 2000-05
(000 Hectares)

District	*Rice*	*Coconut*	*Rubber*	*Gap*	*Gap after 2% for other crops*
Trivandrum	-20.11	15.86	17.62	-	-
Kollam	-27.77	-18.98	0.45	46.30	37.04
Alapuzha	-41.45	-8.35	-0.37	50.17	40.14
Kottayam	-19.12	-16.63	52.30	-	-
Idukki	-11.18	4.90	21.15	-	-
Ernakulam	38.99	13.17	33.73	-	-
Trichur	64.28	23.89	11.26	12.63	10.10
Palakkad	34.21	26.70	16.74	-	-
Malappuram	46.80	32.78	8.67	5.35	4.28
Kozhikode	52.65	22.16	0.34	30.15	24..32
Kannur	67.16	6.38	6.87	53.91	43.12
KERALA	382.27	102.06	169.13	-	158.80

Inter district growth analysis clearly shows that area under rice declined in all the districts between 1975-76 and 2004-05 the fall occurred in Trichur district (64.28 thousand hectares) followed by Kozhikode, Malappuram and Palakkad districts. There is fall in Kannur and Alappuzha districts also, but is due to the division of these districts respectively to Kasaragod and Pathanamthitta. All the districts together made a decline of 382.27 during the time span. Decade wise, the fall is 242.97 thousand hectares between 1975-76 and 1985-86. Hence, based on the estimated growth rates, we may infer that the relative contribution of rice to the total cropped area consistently declined in all the districts in the state, the steep fall being in northern parts.

Naturally, this fall should be reflected in an increase of the area of other crops particularly coconut and rubber felt apriori. In the case of area under coconut, maximum increase is recorded in northern districts, particularly Malappuram (32.78 thousand hectares) and Kozhikode (22.16 thousand hectares between 1975-76 and 2000-01. During the same period Trichur district and Palakkad district respectively recorded an increase of 23.89 thousand hectares and 26.70 thousand hectares. It is important to note that Kollam and Kottayam districts recorded a fall in the area under coconut. During the period 1975-76 to 2000-01, the net increase in the area under coconut in the state is 102.06 thousand hectares, decade wise split ups are (-50.37) thousand hectares and 152.43 thousand hectares. Compared to the fall in the area under rice between 1985-86 and 1999-00 (139.30 thousand hectares). It is seen that the spread in area under coconut is higher than the spread in the case of staple food rice. Hence, growth analysis signifies and reassures that, in the recent years, there is definitely a trend in favour of coconut plantations in northern Kerala.

Kerala state contributed nearly 90 per cent of rubber production in the country. Inter district data reveal that since 1975-76, rubber plantations were extended to all the districts. It is also seen that over the last 25 years, area under rubber cumulatively increased by 169.13 thousand hectares.

An attempt is also made to examine the variations in production and yield with respect to rice, coconut and the inter district levels during the period 1975-76 to 2000-01. Rice production improved from 1067.53 thousand tonnes in 1960-61 to 1364.87 thousand tonnes in 1975-76. Since then it started to decline and the current production (2004) is 2218 kg/hector. The districts which recorded maximum in production are Palakad and Trichur districts of which Palakad district served as the rice bowl of Kerala immediately after the formation of the state in 1956.

The production of coconut increased from 3439 million nuts in 1975-76 to 5895 million nuts in 2004, respective yield being 4962 and 6888. Among the districts, net addition is highest in Kozhikode, Malappuram and Kannur districts followed by Trichur, Palakad, Ernakulam and Trivandrum districts. It is very striking to observe that in Kollam district production came down.

Kerala has the virtual monopoly over production of rubber in the country. In absolute terms, yield improved from 611 kg./hectare in 1975-76 to 1000 in 1999-00 and 1200 in 2001. Leaving home district Kottayam, the other districts made commendable performance of production or rubber area Ernakulam, Trichur, and Trivandrum. The good performance of production and yield is definitely due to the efforts taken by the Rubber Board. But the crucial question is whether the excess supply of rubber in relation to consumption within the state will be able to attract sufficient margins? It is true that still there is wide gap between present production and consumption. But whether the gap will be filled by domestic rubber or imported rubber? These discussions validate our hypothesis that the growth trends in the cropping pattern of Kerala state has turned in favour of cash crops particularly coconut and rubber at the cost of area under rice, the staple food of the state. Thus the pertained question is whether these growth patterns are supplemented and complemented by the growth rates of use of inputs, the price trends and also demand.

Farm Credit

The farm credit is provided by three agencies namely commercial banks, Regional Rural Banks and Co-operatives. Available data reveal that in 1988-89, the total farm credit disbursed in Kerala stood at Rs. 530.40 crores, of which the share of commercial banks being 55 per cent, RRBs 8.4 per cent and cooperative banks 36.00 per cent. In 1992-93 these shares stood respectively at 45.20 per cent, 11 per cent and 43.80 per cent. Over a period of five years the share of cooperatives substantially improved. But this improvement was only temporary. In the immediate year, the share of cooperatives steeply falls to 35.96 per cent and the fall continued. In 1999-00, total farm credit accounted Rs. 2431.72 corers; commercial banks credit stood at Rs. 1153.9 crores followed by RRBs (Rs. 211.51) and Cooperative Banks (Rs. 782.11 crores). The statistics suggest that while the credit flow to the farm sector increased by 2.51 times between 1990-00, the share of cooperatives increased only by 2.15 times during the same period. For RRBs and commercial banks the respective figures are 3.60 and 2.55. These results create an impression that cooperative banks, mainly created for the services of agricultural sector are moving from their primary objective with a shift from agricultural lending to non-agricultural lending.

The credit flow to primary sector spatially also showed desperate picture among the districts ranging from Rs. 24.23 crore in Kollam to Rs. 56.97 crore in Kozhikode during 1999-00. Some districts had lesser credit flow in the primary sector on a per hectare basis compared to the state average of Rs. 4500 crores (approximately). The credit flow to the primary sector had no direct relation to the CD ratio in various districts. Kollam, Idukki and Wayanad with a CD ratio of 67 per cent, 79 per cent and 101 per cent had per hectare credit of Rs. 2423, Rs. 3284 and Rs. 4076 respectively as compared to Trivandrum (Rs. 5929), Kottayam (Rs. 5498) and Kannur (Rs. 4353) with CD ratio of 37 per cent, 42 per cent and 31 per cent respectively.

Now turning to the trends in investment credit to agriculture sector, it is seen that in 1988-89 investment credit stood at Rs. 142.10 crore, the share in the total agriculture credit being 26.79 per cent. Over a period of 12 years this multiplied by just 0.74 times, the share in total agricultural credit in 1999-00 being 12.74 per cent. On the other hand production credit (Short-term and medium-term) recorded an increase of 2.62 times. The trends infer that the flow of credit is poor and stagnant. Despite commercialization of agriculture as seen in the recent past, term-loan per net cropped area averaged only around Rs. 700 per annum. Considering the predominance of capital intensive perennial crops in the cropping system practiced in Kerala the average investment is low and raises several concerns. They include the following.

The major trends revealed from the pattern of institutional finance for agriculture in Kerala in recent years are the following.

1. There is a claim in Kerala, particularly by the bankers that there is no credit gap in the state. This claim is invalid because the scale of finance norms create the real problem in reducing the credit gap.

2. The proportion of finance made available to the farm front is on the decline. (see Tables 7 and 8).
3. Short term credit predominates the farm credit advance, accounting for more than 75 per cent of the total. In the context of the structural transformation taking place in the farm front of Kerala in favour of perennial crops, the importance of production credit is diminishing and the need for term loan is increasing. However, this is not reflected in the credit font.
4. The average per hectare credit advanced continues to be low both in respect of short term as well as long term.

Table 7
Annual Credit Flow to Agriculture in Kerala During 1997-98 to 2004-05RS crore

	1997-98	*1998-99*	*1999-00*	*2004-05*
Commercial banks	831.33	1153.98	1318.55	3884
	(39.23)	(42.86)	(39.28)	(32.71)
Regional Rural Banks	196.55	211.51	331.06	1066
	(55.56)	(55.44)	(60.08)	(72.36)
Cooperatives	506.24	561.64	782.11	1904
	(53.14)	(49.51)	(46.23)	(38.27)
Grand Total	1534.12	1927.13	2431.72	6854
	(43.00)	(42.67)	(42.16)	(37.27)

Source: SLBC Figures in italics are percentages of priority credit

Table 8
Flow of Credit to Agriculture in Kerala as a Proportion of Credit and Deposits (in %)

Year	*As a % of total credit*	*As a % of total deposits*
1991	17.4	10.3
1993	15.7	7.5
1995	15.4	6.9
1997	15.2	6.2
1999	14.4	6.2
2000	13.9	5.8
2005	17.4	9.4

Source: SLBC

These arguments lead to the inference that the growth in agricultural credit growth in terms of demand and disbursement is only quantitative and not qualitative.

Fertilisers

Table 9 explains the growth in the use of chemical fertilizers in Kerala. It is seen that until late 1980s, the use of chemical fertilizers was very minimum in Kerala; per hectare use was only 16.13 kg. in 1960-61 and 19.10 kg. in 1970-71. In 1990-91, the use went up to 203000 tonnes, the per hectare use being 66.62 kg. In 2001-02, the volume of use declined and this is due to reduction in area under crops; but the per hectare use increased to 76.25 kg. But these usage rates are low compared to the average rate in certain other countries. Again the important question is not that whether per hectare use is high or low but whether the use is efficient or not? Mere increase in physical quantity will not ensure quality.

Table 9
Consumption of Fertilizers in Kerala

Year	*Consumption 000 Tonnes*	*Per Hect (kg)*
1960-61	58	16.13
1970-71	77	19.17
1980-81	94	32.84
1990-91	203	66.62
1995-96	203	58.13
2000-01	173	76.25
2004-05	192	74.28

Source: Economic Review, Government of Kerala.

IRRIGATION FACILITIES

The use of chemical fertilizers and the area under irrigation are highly correlated. In 1960-61, the gross irrigated area came to 456.25 thousand hectares and net irrigated area 218.00 thousand hectares. These areas respectively increased to 466,000 hectares and 357.000 hectares in 1997-98. In absolute terms the change is only marginal but this is due to a total reduction in area under crops. Net irrigated area as per cent of net sown area which stood at 16.57 per cent in 1960-61 improved to 40.98 per cent in 1997-98. (See Table 10). Discussions establish that the priority given to irrigation in recent years is insignificant compared to previous decades.

Table 10
Irrigated Area Kerala (000 hect)

Year	*Gorss Irrigated Area*	*Net Irrigated Area*	*Net Irrigated Areaas % of Nsa*
1960-61	456.25	318	16.57
1970-71	601.38	431	20.50
1980-81	380.90	237.90	22.61
1990-91	383	333	14.84
1995-98	466	342	15.10
1997/98	466	357	20.98
2003-04	426	381	17.38

Source: Economic Survey Government of Kerala.

Subsidies

The subsidy till accruing towards agriculture is going up though the general impression is that all subsidies have been pruned in recent years. Budgetary subsidies for the agriculture sector have been increasing in nominal terms over the years. The share of fertilizer subsidies in the total subsidies of the central government steadily increased from 35 per cent in 1980s to 42 per cent in the first half of the 1990s and further to 49.80 per cent in the second half. In absolute terms, it rose from Rs. 4390 crores during 1900-00. Power sector subsidies to agriculture account for over one per cent of GDP. Hidden subsidies provided by the states for agriculture increased from Rs. 5938 crores in 1991-92 to Rs. 25577 crores in 1999-00. These evidences invalidate the hypothesis that globalisation and resultant reforms restricted subsides.

The discussions reassured the claim that, over the years, in absolute terms the increase in the use of inputs was significant. At the same time, the significant increase in use of inputs is not directly reflected in the output growth. This may be due to two reasons or more. One probable explanation is that the growth in output is not well reflected and revealed due to leakages including distribution. Another proposition is that, the out put is not receiving fair and reasonable price. It is well accepted that the problem of escalating input prices and stagnating output prices is crippling the performance of agriculture sector.

The above discussions establish that the agriculture growth performance of the Kerala state is not uniform spatially and inter temporally. Hence it is recommended to have a revamped vision to dress the sector to absorb the implications and consequences of globalisation and reforms.

N. RADHAKRISHNAN

Food Security in India: Post Reform Scenario

4

INTRODUCTION

The issues related to livelihood and food security remain critical for a country like India, owing to the fact that majority of population still depends on agriculture for employment and income. Agriculture has been with the Indian population for the last 10,000 years as a way of life, lively hood and part of Social system. The emergence of W.T.O. which was instrumental in signing several global trade related agreements, created a series of positive and negative impact upon the over all performance of the agricultural sector. An array of challenges is at the threshold of Indian agricultural sector. Among these challenges the issues related to ensuring physical and financial accessibility to reasonable and sufficient quantities of food has become a prime concern in front of the present government. The recent political polarization at the center has sharpened the focus on this vital issue in the midst of the mounting agrarian distress of the last two years.0Food security has been accepted as one of the principal goals of development because of the close link between food security and poverty alleviation. A recent Food and Agricultural Organization (FAO) Study shows that, about 23 per cent of total population (225 million people) are undernourished and about 24 per cent of total population (260 million people) are below the poverty line. Although the number of people below poverty line has reduced significantly between 1993-94 and 1999-2000, the number of undernourished people has increased during the period 1992-1999.

The world agricultural trade scenario underwent dramatic changes under the smoke of W.T.O's most controversial agreement known as Agreement on Agriculture (AoA). The implementation of AoA was supposed to bring a structural change in the world food grains market. It was expected that due to the reduction commitments of the developed countries, cereal production would shift from highly subsidized regions to low-subsidized regions. However the reality is that there has not been much change in the pattern of world cereals production and exports. This can be attributed to the fact that there have not been any significant reduction in the aggregate domestic transfers to the agriculture sector in most developed countries. It was our expectation that due to the committed reduction in subsidies by developed countries, the world prices of agriculture commodities would increase. However contrary to expectations prices of most agricultural commodities declined globally. The trade distorting agricultural subsidies given by developed countries to their farmers to support the unsustainable agriculture sector created much problem to our farming community.

The world food security situation itself is looking bleak. The Indian food security scenario also gives some alarming signals. Population growth rate and higher percapita income necessitate a growing demand for food grains. However the supply scenario shows a mismatch between increased demand and reduced supply. The economic incentives are inducing farmers towards the cultivation of cash crops. The yield growth rate of food grains is stagnating in most parts of India. Based on these facts various studies have pointed out that India is going to be a net importer of rice in near future. For wheat, some surplus production will continue to exist in the near future. India is not currently globally competitive in wheat. However in the case of rice she is comfortably placed in the global market. But due to radical shift in cropping pattern, the surplus production of rice is going to be eroded very soon. The implication is that there is every probability for India to become import dependent in food grains particularly in rice in the near future. Moreover the opening up of agriculture trade will push up prices of rice in the domestic market. International rice prices are significantly higher than domestic price of rice. Therefore in the short run, domestic prices will tend to go up as more exports take place. Rice is the main staple food of Indian population and any rise in price of rice will affect the poor adversely. Hence agricultural trade liberalization may badly affect the poor in terms of non-availability of foodstuffs at affordable price.

India has managed to develop one of the worlds most extensive government managed food grains distribution system. Still the availability of food grains in terms of quantity as well as quality is uneven among different sections of the Society. This is reflected also in the paradoxical co occurrence of high food grains inventories in the government coffers and starvation deaths. Besides the incidence of malnutrition is also fairly high.

Distribution of food at subsidized prices has been accepted for long, an integral part of the public policy by most countries of the world, due to the realization that famines are caused not because of the non-availability of food, but because of entitlement failure also. Wide spread unemployment and the resulting acute mass poverty are the crucial problems facing the Indian society. Hunger is the extreme manifestation of poverty. In a paradoxically complex society of India, there are millions who go to bed hungry in spite of millions of tones of food grains dumped in the warehouses.

Poor people are witnessing extreme form of deprivation resulting in chronic hunger, malnutrition and starvation deaths. Public provisioning is far from adequate. Under the targeted P.D.S. which was meant to serve the families below poverty line, each poor family irrespective of size and need is entitled uniform quantity of 100 Kg. of food grains per family per month. Contrary to government claim about food availability in P.D.S. outlets, its functionary is irregular, corrupt and at times the prices are beyond the reach of the starving population. This is reflected in the high incidence of poverty and malnutrition among the rural population in India. Poor remains poor because they have no productive assets and there is no value for their time. Against this background, this paper is a modest attempt to analyze the concept of food security and the emerging issues in food stock management.

FOOD SECURITY: CONCEPTS AND MEASUREMENT

Food security as a concept originated only in the mid 1970s, in the discussion of International food problems at a time of global food crisis. The early focus of attention was primarily on food supply problems. The issues of famine, hunger and food crisis were also being extensively examined; following the events of the mid 1970s . The outcome was a redefinition of food security, which recognized the fact that the behaviour of potentially vulnerable and affected people was a crucial aspect. Food security is an important issue where millions of people are hungry and poverty stricken. The inability of a person to eat enough food, stay active and lead a healthy life comes under the preview of food insecurity (Food Insecurity Atlas of India 2001). The World Bank defined food security as "access by all people at all times to enough food for an active and healthy life" (W.B. 1986. P. 39). The scope of the concept was broadened at the World Food Summit held in Rome in 1996 by declaring that food security exists when all people at all times have physical and economic access to sufficient, safe and nutritive food to meet the dietary needs and food preference for active and healthy life (FAO. 1996). In this definition both physical accessibility as well as economic access was considered. The World Food Summit also gave importance for the food security of the poor. P.D.S. is one of the most significant means of ensuring physical access to food. Physical access is meaningless, in case where economic access is missing. Besides, mere physical availability of food grains is of little value if not accompanied with availability of potable drinking water, hygienic living conditions, and proper health care. But these elements are not addressed by the P.D.S. in India.

As defined, household food security depends on adequate income and assets, including cultivable land-owned and/or leased-which ensures that each household is able to produce or procure the food it needs. The root cause of household food insecurity is poverty. All poor people have inadequate access to natural resources, jobs, incomes or social support. Hence professor Saminathan and Prof. Amarthya Sen opines that food security is a broader concept and it depends upon a number of factors like availability, affordability, income distribution, poverty alleviation programme etc.

Hence food security symbolizes a situation where everyone has access at all times to food needed for an active and healthy life. Thus the essential elements of food security are (a) adequate availability of food (b) availability of adequate purchasing power in the hands of the people and (c) efficient distribution through public distribution system.

THE PARADOX IN FOOD SECURITY

Food security issue in any country depends on a wide range of factors. The important among them are domestic food demand, changing food preference, domestic production, net availability, effectiveness of poverty alleviation programmes etc. Emerging food security scenario in India is examined in terms of some of these critical determinants.

DOMESTIC REQUIREMENTS

There are a number of projections showing the population growth and food requirements in India. According to an official estimate, the country's populations which has already crossed one billion mark, is likely to rise to 1.16 billion by 2010, and 1.6 billion by 2050. To feed these additional mouths, the country's food grains output will have to be stepped up substantially to around 247 million tones by 2010 and over 320 million tones by 2050. However the present output level ranges between 200-210 Mt. on an average. This seems an uphill task, difficult to realize.

In 2004-05 the food production in India was only 204.6 million tones. The first advance estimate of food grains production for 2005-06, released by Ministry of Agriculture on September 19, 2005, put Kharif production at 105.3 Mt., up by 2 Mt. from previous year. Production of Rabi food grains is estimated around last year level of 101.3 Mt. provided weather condition remains the same. (Economic Survey, 2005-06, page 157). An analysis of trend in food production from 1998-99 to 2004-05 clearly shows that actual production fell short of targeted production. (Table 1)

Table 1
Food Grains Production: Target & Actual (in Mt.)

Year	*Target*	*Achieved*
1998-99	210	203
99-2000	209	209.8
00-01	212	196.8
01-02	218	212.9
02-03	220	174.8
03-04	240	213.5
04-05	NA	204.6

Source: Economic Survey, 2005-06, page 157.

This declining trend in domestic production can be attributed to inadequate irrigation cover, improper adoption of agricultural technology, weakness in credit delivery system, shift in cropping pattern towards high value commercial crops and decline in public investment in critical agricultural infrastructure. In such a situation to step up food production in tune with growing mouths, seems an uphill task, difficult to realize.

Per Capita Production

Per Capital food production is a very critical factor in ensuring food and nutritional security. Per Capita food production is linked with total food production and technology used in production. In India the technology adoption rare in agriculture is only thirty per cent. Majority of Indian Farmers are still depending on the fate of weather for cultivation. Data on Per Capita food production In India shows that it is on a declining trend. In 1991–92, net output per head was 178.77 Kg. per year. It dropped to 150.09 Kg. Per year in 2002-03. (Usha Patnaik, 2004).

Table 2
Per Capita Food Grains Production Scenario

Year	*Net Per Capital Production (Kg/Yr)*
1991 - 92	178.77
2000 - 01	167.43
2001 - 02	177.01
2002 - 03	150-09

Source: Usha Patnaik: Food Stock & Hunger, Social Scientist, July-August-2004.

Per Capita Availability

This is another important aspect of food security. Per Capita availability depends on Per capita production. When per capita production declines, per capita availability also declines. Another crucial factor determining per capita availability is the purchasing power in the hands of the people. Reductions in per capita availability adversely effect the nutrition requirement of the people. Available data shows that in 1991-92 the net per capita availability was 177 Kg./year. It dropped to 150.09 Kg./year in 2002-03. (Usha Patnaik, 20).

Table 3
Food Grains Availability Scenario.

Year	Net per capita Availability Kg./Yr.
1991-92	177.00
2000-01	151.06
2001-02	158.37
2002-03	150.09

Source: Usha Patnaik: Food Stock & Hunger, Social Scientist, July-August-2004.

Sufficient purchasing power.

Adequate purchasing power in the hands of the people is the most important factor determining food security. More production and buffer stock creation will not solve the food problem. The people should posses sufficient money to purchase the food stuffs provided through ration shops at subsidized rates.

Change in Food Prefere

Food security also means that people should get adequate food items according to their preference. In India the fall in Calorie-in-take of cereals and increased calories-in-take of supplementary food like fruits, vegetables, fish meat, egg etc shows the changing food preference of the people. Hence food security should take into consideration, the changes taking place in peoples food preference overtime due to change in their income and standard of living.

Scientific Management of Food Stock

Food stock management is a crucial factor determining the food security issue. Food security is closely linked with food grains trading policy as well as food stock management. The main elements of food grains policy consist of restrictions on free export, canalized imports through State agencies and procurement policy. The elements of food stock management consists of adequate buffer stock creation of food grains, its proper distribution to the poor population and scientific management of the distributions system.After independence, in India public distribution was deemed as the most important instrument for ensuring food security at household level as it could provide economic and physical access to food. During the post independence period PDS in India continued to grow in both scope and coverage. Revamped public distribution system (RPDS) was introduced in 1992 to supply PDS commodities to the people living in backward hilly land tribal areas. From June 1997, the Govt. of India introduced Targeted public distribution system (TPDS).

Where dual central issue price (CIP), one for the B.P.L. household and another for the APL households was introduced to benefit the poor (BPL families) and to curtail food subsidies over a period. The food grains were released from the central pool ie. FCI to the State Govt. on the basis of the number of persons below poverty line as estimated by the Planning Commission, Government of India.

FLAWS IN INDIA'S FOOD SECURITY SYSTEM

At the time of independence, India faced two major nutritional problems; one was the threat of famine and acute starvation due to lack of national and regional food security system; the other was chronic under nutrition due to low dietary intake, because of lack of purchasing power among the poorer segments of population. The first effect of the country was to build up a food security system to ensure that the thread of famine no longer stalks the country. The policy package employed to achieve food security consisted of institutional changes like land reforms and huge investments in agriculture. Within this framework the green revolution technology was popularized and emphasized through cheap and subsidized inputs to ensure food security. These measures were supplemented and complemented with a positive price policy for food grains producers and ensuring food grains availability through P.D.S. for consumers. The fact that the country has not witnessed famine and acute starvation on a massive scale in the last five decades, since the inception of centralized planning and control is the most eloquent testimony for the success of these efforts. But this success story is not universally applicable to all Indians. The under privileged people have faced food in security at different times and space.

In the wake of structural reforms introduced since 1991 with a view to trimming government size and reducing fiscal deficit, the approach of Govt. of India towards PDS, underwent a drastic change. Since then Govt. of India has become more concerned with reducing food subsidies rather than supplying food at subsidized price to the population and with efficient functioning of the market rather than interfering with the market through regulation and controls, revamped public distribution system was replaced by targeted public distribution system. The Economic reforms initiated in early 1990's have far-reaching implication on agriculture export and imports, investment in agriculture and rural development. This in turn effects growth rates and its patterns, income and employment in agriculture and agriculture price and food security. The problem of food security, in particular, is bound to assume growing importance due to the increasing size of Indian population and its growth rate, withdrawal of subsidies on essential inputs like electricity, fertilizer etc. which may adversely effect agricultural output, fiscal correctness in the spirit of structural adjustment and yearly fluctuating food grains production (Bhalla 1994) The foregone analysis clearly pin points to some basic concerns which affects the Indian food security scenario.

Mismatch between food Grains Production and Population Growth

A critical analyze of food security scenario, makes it imperative to analyze the emerging demand for and supply of food grains. Demand for food grains can be analyzed from the trend in population growth rate. Supply of food grains can be analyzed from the trend in food grains growth rate. (Table 4).

Table 4
Growth Rates of food Grains and Population During 1990's
(in % per year)

Period	*Food grains*	*Population Growth*
1980 - 81 to 1989 - 1990	2.85	2.1
1990 - 1991 to 2000 - 01	1.66	1.9

Source: Economic Survey, 2001-02, pp. 189.

The table clearly shows that the decade 1980's witnessed the fastest food grains production growth ever since the green revolution (i.e. 2.85% per annum). The decade 1990's could not maintain that tempo. Consequently; the food grains output growth rate fell from 2.85% per year to 1.66% in 1990. This is less than the population growth rate of 1.9%. As a result per head net food grains output had fallen considerably. Coupled with this the area under production of food grains has also fallen from 125 million hectors in 1998–99 to 113 Mh in 2002-03. Due to change in cropping pattern, now in India, more area is diverted for the cultivation of high value crops like plantation crops, floriculture, sericulture etc. The following table illustrates this point clear. (Table 5).

Table 5
Area under Production of Food Grains
(In Million Hectors)

Year	*Area (M.H.)*
1998 - 99	125.17
1999 - 2000	123.10
2000 - 01	121.05
2001 - 02	121.91
2002 - 03	113.13

Source: Economic Survey: 2003-04.

This declining trend in area used for food crops cultivation considerably affected food grains production. Hence due to population growth, demand for food grains shows an increasing trend, where as due to technological and changes in cropping structure, food grains production and supply increases slowly. The technology adoption rate is 30% as far as the agricultural sector is concerned. This mismatch between demand for and supply of food grains creates serious problem in our food security system.

Paradox in Food Grains Availability and Consumption

India, as stated earlier, has managed to develop one of the worlds most extensive Govt. managed food grains distribution system. Still the availability of food grains in terms of quantity as well as quality is uneven among different sections of the society. This is reflected in the co-existence of high food grains stock in the Government coffers and starvation deaths.

Production of food grains in sufficient quantity is necessary but not sufficient for providing food security. For achieving food security, the availability of food grains is important. Availability in turn is determined by the purchasing power of the people. People should possess sufficient money to purchase the food grains provided through the P.D.S.

In India there is a large build up of public food stocks over the last four years. As on January 2005, the buffer stock sitting idle with the Food Corporation of India go downs was 21.7 Million tones. This was higher than the buffer stock norms of 16.8 Mt. Food grains stock have however remained consistently higher than the buffer stock requirements during the ten months of 2004-05(Economic Survey, 2004-05). The excess stock over and above the buffer norms is an indication of the availability problem among the marginalized communities and poor rural households. Reduction in purchasing power of the rural poor reduced their absorption of food grains. During the period 1998-2002, nearly 3210 suicide deaths were recorded among the poor farmers of Andrapradesh. During the four years from 2001, over 1250 suicides are recorded in wayanad district in Kerala, when the price to the local growers of coffee, tea and spices have come down drastically than global price. Reduced income and deprivation among the farmers made them poverty stricken and hungry. This paradox is a stack reflection of the comprehensive macro economic mismanagement by the government in following policies that have reduced the purchasing power of people and reduced their absorption of food items.

All food insecure people are poor and unemployed. There is inequality in access to food in Indian society over the last 5 years. Accessibility problem has two dimensions. Physical accessibility and financial accessibility. Physical accessibility in turn depends on increasing population requirement and per capita production. The declining trend in total food production and low percapita output lead to reduced physical accessibility of food items. However mere physical accessibility cannot ensure food security. It should be supplemented by financial accessibility i.e. adequate income to purchase the subsidized food items distributed through P.D.S. The food absorption level in India is comparatively very low. During the period 1950-55, the net availability of food items per head was 152 kg./year. Owing to the impact of green revolution and interventionist policies in the distribution system, the net availability reached to 177 Kg./year during the period 1989-91. However in the post reform period this absorption level declined drastically. Estimates shows that on an average during the period 200-01 and 2001-02, the net availability per head was only 155.15 Kg./ year.

The reduced net availability of food items among the poor rural folk can be attributed to another important factor i.e. Reduced income and purchasing power. Factors like (a) Reduced public expenditure on rural development activities and high incidence of rural indebtedness led to reduced rural employment, reduced rural income and high incidence of poverty in rural areas. (b) Coupled with this sharply falling farm price for commercial crops both globally and locally from 1996-97 onwards also contributed towards reducing the disposable income of the farmers.

A closer analysis of the employment scenario in India shows that the annual rate of growth of employment has declined considerably from 2.04 per cent per annum during 1983-94 to 0.98 per cent per annum during 1994-2000. A sectoral analysis of the phenomenon reveals that even in the reform period agricultural sector had experienced decline in the annual rate of growth of employment. The rate of growth of employment in the agricultural sector was 1.51% during 1983–94, where as it registered in a negative growth rate (-) 0.34% during 1994-2000. This has worsened the situation in rural India and only helped to mound up the agrarian stress.

Public investment in rural development activities usually help to provide a supplementary source of income to the farmer community during times of crop failure and off farm activities. However an analysis of the structure and pattern of rural development expenditure in 1990s shows that it has been declining continuously over the years. This has contributed towards reduced disposable income to the farmers and aggravated the incidence of hunger and poverty among the rural farm households. The composition of public investment in agriculture is on a declining trend in the reform period. The volume of total public gross fixed capital formation referred to as public investment, on an annual average, works out to be Rs. 6050/- Crores (1999 – 94 prices) during the period 78–79 to 89-90. This drastically declined to Rs. 4293/- crores for 1990-91 to 1999-2000. (Table 6).

Table 6
Public Development Expenditure in Rural Areas in Nineties
(As % of G.D.P.)

Year	*1985-90*	*1991-92*	*1995-96*	*1997-98*	*2000-01*
Rural Development. Expenditure as % of G.D.P.	14.5	11.7	6.0	5.6	5.9

NB: Rural Development expenditure include expenditure on agriculture, rural dept, special area programme, irrigation and flood control, village industry, energy and transport. (Usha Patnaik, Social Scientist, July-August, 2004).

Continuous declining trend in public investment directly affects agriculture. It leads to a declining trend in the creations of infrastructure facilities, agricultural production, employment and income generation and ultimately the affordability of food items.

Along with this the sharp fall in the prices of commercial crops globally and locally, after 1996, reduced the income of the rural people. Globally primary prices were rising up to 1996. Thereafter it went into a prolonged decline. Between 1995 and 2001, the fall in unit dollar price of cereals, cotton, sugar and jute was 40 per cent to 50 per cent. There occurred even 85 per cent decline in some edible oil prices. Coupled with this the percentage share of agricultural export in total export also started declining. In 1990-91 it was 19% and it dipped to 9.6% in 2005-06 (April to October). In the light of AoA, our agricultural exports became conditioned by a number of domestic and multilateral issues, which are beyond the control of our poor farmers. The distorted support systems coupled with heavy subsidy provided by developed countries to their farm sector only helped to reduce the export earnings of our farmers. This reduced agricultural exports contributed to a considerable fall in export earnings of majority of farmers in rural areas and reduced disposable income to the farming community.

Farmer indebtedness has been singled out as the foremost cause for farmer suicides and food insecurity problems. A recently published data based on a comprehensive survey covering 51770 farmer households spread over 6638 villages conducted by NSSO (59th Round) pinpoints to the massive indebtedness among farmer households, being a major cause for agrarian distress. The survey data shows that the proportion of households reporting indebtedness at all India level was 25.90% in the year 1991-92. It increased to 48.60% in 2003. Across analysis of the data shows that the incidence of indebtedness are very high in the States of Andra Pradesh (82%), followed by Tamil Nadu (74%), Kerala (65) and Karnataka (60%). The average debt per household at constant price also has shown an increase of 210% during the period under consideration. In 1991-92 it was Rs. 1254/- and it increased to Rs. 3884/- by 2003. A catogorywise analysis shows that OBC, SC, and ST category households constitute 72% of the indebted farmer households. Moreover 70% indebted farmers own less than two hectors of land. A purpose wise analysis of datedness shows that 50% of borrowing accrue to meet consumption needs of farmer households.

We have seen that provision of minimum nutritional support to the poor through subsidized food grains and ensuring price stability for agricultural products are the twin objectives of food security system. By fulfilling the obligations towards ensuring distributive justice, the government incurs food subsidies. Food subsidies showed an annual increase of about 27% during each of the 3 years–2000-01, 2001-02 and 2002-03. However the annual increase came down to 4.1% during 2003-04 and is expected to further decelerate to 2.54% in 2004-05(Economic Survey, 2005-06).

CONCLUSION

Public distribution system targeted towards the needy is the most effective means of ensuring physical access to food for the marginalized rural households. But mere physical access is rendered immaterial in case where economic access is missing. Mounting rural indebtedness and reduced farm income of rural households deprive them from accessing the subsidized food stuffs distributed through Public Distribution system. This is reflected in the paradoxical co-existence of high food grains inventories in the government coffers and starvation deaths. This is a major concern, which necessitates immediate public intervention. Macro stabilization policy under the rubric of NEP, initiated in non-farm sectors failed to percolate economic prosperity to rural areas. The "trickle down effect" had'nt materialized. However Government of India initiated an integrated approach towards rural development under the umbrella of the National Common Minimum Programme. As a result of the implementation of the anti-poverty and employment generation programmes, the situation is slowly changing. The off-take of food grains under TPDS registered an increase from 154.55 lakh tones in April-November 2003 to 265.7 lakh tones during April-November 2005. This is rendered possible due to an all-round improvement in the off-take of food grains under BPL and Antoyada categories of households. The increased flow of institutional credit to agricultural sector also gives an array of hope in solving the agrarian distress and food insecurity problems. In 2000-01, the total volume of institutional credit to agricultural sector was Rs. 52827/-crortes. In the year 2005-06, it increased to 117899/- crores. The government should give more thrust towards enhancing productivity and employment generation in the agricultural sector. Entitlement is the real problem faced by poor farmer households leading to starvation and malnutrition. A reoriented and focused attention towards rural development is the crying need of the hour to ensure food security to the rural households.

REFERENCES

Ashok Gulati (1998), 'Indian Economy in an Open Economy' in India's Economic Reforms and Development Essays for Manmohan Singh, ed. by Isher Judge Aluwalia and IMD Little.

FAO (2001), The State of Food Insecurity in the World, Rome.

World Bank (1986), Poverty and Hunger, Issues and Options for Food Security in Developing Countries, Washington DC.

Government of India (2000), Review of WTO Agreement on Agriculture, New Delhi, Ministry of Agriculture.

Government of India, Economic Survey, Ministry of Finance, Various Issues.

Usha Patnaik, 'Food Stock and Hunger', Social Scientist, July-August, 2004.

World Trade Organization (2002), 'Trade Policy Review, India, GATT, Geneva.

Singh, S. (2002), "Rural Credit in India: Some Concerns" in Acharya S.S., Singh S. and Sagar V. (eds.) Sustainable Agriculture, Poverty and Food Security: Agenda for Asian Economies, Rawat Publications, Jaipur and New Delhi.

Rao, C.H.H. & Gulati, A.(1994), "Indian Agriculture, Emerging Perspectives and Major Policy issues" Economic & Political Weekly, 29 (53).

Dantwala, M.L. and others (Collection of Essays): *India's Agricultural Development since Independence*, Oxford and IBH.

Aditya Bhattacharya, *India's Competition Policy, An Assessment*, Economic & Political Weekly, August 2-29, 2003.

Govinda, Rao M. & Misra, V.N., *Trade Policy, Agricultural Growth and Rural Poor, Economic & Political Weekly*, October-25, 2003.

Vasudeva, P.K. (2005), "World Trade Organization: Implication for Indian Economy", Pearson Education, New Delhi.

PART - IV
Finance and External Sector

U. RAMACHANDRAN

Post Reform Fiscal Trends in India

5

It is about one and half decade since economic reforms were introduced in India so vigorously in the context of liberalization, privatisation and globalisation. Among many other macro-management stabilisation policies, Fiscal consolidation is a necessary pre-requisite for sustained growth. The fiscal performance of the States in India and the Central Government is under great pressure. In a developing economy like India, where a significant proportion of people remain poor and rural, subsidies are an essential component of expenditures.

The years 1990 and 1991 are important landmark years in the post-independent India. Huge budgetary deficit, alarming growth of wholesale prices (6.6 per cent), slow down in GDP growth, low industrial output, negative agricultural growth and many other constraints paused the economic growth processes. The balance of payments was under strain and foreign exchange reserves were down to around Rs.5000 crore and stock of food grains had fallen to 11 million tonnes. Prof Madhu Dandavate, the then Finance Minister in his 1990-91 budget speech cautioned about the fiscal imbalance as the root cause of the twin problems of inflation and the difficult balance of payment position. Dr. Manmohan Singh's maiden budget of 1991-92, reiterated the accentuation of fiscal imbalances, Gulf crisis, great weakening of international confidence and sharp decline in capital inflows through commercjal borrowing and non-resident deposits.

The record borrowing from international Monetary Fund(IMF) in July 1990 and January 1991 resulted in a sharp reduction in our foreign exchange reserves. The foreign exchange crisis threatened the sustainability of growth process and orderly implementation of our development programmes. The major reasons attributed was the persistent macro-economic imbalances and the low productivity of investment, in particular the poor rates of return on past investments. There has been an unsustainable increase in government expenditure. Budgetary subsidies, with questionable social and economic impact have been allowed to grow to an alarming extent. The felt emergency was a credible fiscal adjustment and macro-economic stabilization which includes progressive reduction in the fiscal deficit, a significant reduction in the revenue deficit, curbing the exponential growth in internal and external debt and limiting the burden of debt servicing to manageable levels.

The New Economic policy of India has not necessarily diminished the role of state according to Dr. C. Rangarajan. It has only redefined it, expanding it in some areas and reducing in some others. As it has been said, somewhat paradoxically " more market" does not mean "less government", but only "different government". The development experience of our country have shown that there can be both government failure and market failure and that the critical issue is not so much the presence or absence of state intervention, but the extent and quality of that intervention.

ECONOMIC STRENGTH

The Gross Domestic Product (GDP at current prices) which was Rs. 5,10,954 crore in 1990-91 increased to Rs. 9,17,058 crore in 1994-95 and further to Rs. 25,19,785 crore in 2003-04. These increases are 16.7,17.4 and 11.7. It is estimated to increase by 12.6 per cent in 2004-05 over the previous year and estimated at Rs. 2838123 crore. The Net State Domestic Product at All India level shows increases of 17.3 per cent in 1994-95 over the previous year, 10.4 per cent in 1999-2000 and 12.1 per cent in 2003-04 over the previous years. A latest estimate of GDP growth expected is 7.6 per cent during 2005-06 and expected to reach Rs. 3045618 crores. The GDP grew by 8.1 per cent in the first half of 2005-06. Manufacturing sector grew by 9.9 per cent and the services sector maintained the growth momentum with 12.2 per cent. The trend in Net State Domestic Product of the selected few states indicates that almost all States could not achieve the growth rate of 1994-95 in the subsequent years. The 17.3 per cent growth rate in 1994-95 had declined to 10.5 per cent in 1999-2000 and further to 8.5 per cent in 2002-03 at the all India level (Table 1) In Kerala the NSDP growth of 21.7 per cent in 1994-95 declined in all the subsequent years and reached at 8.7 per cent growth in 2003-04 over the previous year. The State economy (Kerala) exhibited a high time growth rate of 9.3 per cent, mainly on account of the targeted growth rate of 13.8 per cent in the services sector during 2004-05.

Table 1
Net State Domestic Product

(Rupees crore)

Sl. No.	*States*	*1994-95*	*1999-00*	*2002-03*	*2003-04*
1.	Andhra Pradesh	61789 (19.6)	112966 (8.7)	145198 (6.5)	162153 (11.7)
2.	Bihar	23630 (13.7)	38178 (9.6)	48633 (15.3)	50381 (3.6)
3.	Gujarat	56003 (31.6)	92280 (2.8)	118513 (17.9)	142559 (20.3)
4.	Karnataka	43065 (16.4)	84696 (7.5)	106980 (10.5)	118329 (10.6)
5	Kerala	29022 (21.7)	56944 (11.6)	73697 (13.6)	80116 (8.7)
6	Maharashtra	116507 (14.5)	216641 (16.2)	260812 (10.9)	294001 (12.7)
7	Punjab	30528 (12.8)	54257 (9.4)	64094 (2.7)	69841 (9.0)
8	Tamil Nadu	61276 (18.7)	112554 (6.5)	137788 (8.1)	148907 (8.5)
9	West Bengal	56265 (16.3)	116899 (10.1)	152084 (7.6)	113674 (14.2)
10	All India	819064 (17.3)	1579479 (10.5)	2021936 (8.5)	2266148 (12.1)

*Figures in parenthesis are percentage increase over the previous year.

BUDGET STRAINS

The combined receipts and disbursements of the Central and State Governments indicate the fiscal health of the nation and it reflects on the efforts on the anvil initiated especially in the post reform era. The combined receipts and disbursements of the Central and State Governments show some interesting features of fiscal management and consolidation. In the case of total receipts including tax and non-tax receipts it shows declines in the budget estimates for 2005-06 over the previous year's revised accounts. The higher increase of non-debt capital receipts in the years 2002-03 and 2003-04 was mainly due to the disinvestment proceeds. The declines in the receipts have its impact on the disbursements also. The disbursements on the developmental item considerably less when compared to the non-developmental of which the interest payment is predominantly visible. The disbursements on capital head shows historical increase in 2002-03 and 2003-04 and it is due to repayments of internal debt by the states. It also includes repayments by the centre to the National Small Savings Fund (NSSF) of Rs. 13,766 crore, Rs.46,602 crore and Rs. 32,665 crore respectively in 2002-03, 2003-04 and 2004-05 (Table 2).

The total receipts grew on an average to the extent of 12.1 per cent in 2002-03 and 15.7 per cent in 2003-04. The revised estimates for 2004-05 and budget estimate for 2005-06 shows further declines. The Gross Fiscal Deficit estimated at Rs. 267872 crore for, 2005-06 an increase of 44.9 per cent when compared to 1999-2000, 34.0 per cent to 2000-01 and 3.8 per cent to 2004-05. The GFD has been financed by market borrowing (domestic) to the maximum extent in all these years. The proportions are 44.9 per cent in 1999-2000, 56.5 per cent in 2002-03 and 44.9 per cent in 2005-06 respectively. The other instruments are small savings, reserve funds, deposits and advances, treasury bills excluding 364 day Treasury Bills and loans from financial institutions. The increase in developmental expenditure during 2003-04 was evident across most State Governments, Non-developmental expenditure, as a ratio to GDP, also maintained its steady upward trend to 6.4 per cent of GDP in 2003-04. The ratio of non-developmental expenditure to GSDP was relatively high in the case of many States like Bihar, Orissa, Punjab and Uttar Pradesh. Within non-developmental expenditure, interest payments absorbed over 25 per cent of revenue receipts at the consolidated level. But at the individual State level the situation is worst.

Table 2
Combined Receipts and Disbursements of the Central and State Governments

(Amount in crore)

Item	*1999-00*	*2002-03*	*2003-04*	*2004-05*	*2005-06*
I Total Receipts	5,36,446	7,31,763 (12.1)	8,46,551 (15.7)	9,40,127 (11.1)	9,94,604 (5.8)
A. Revenue Receipts	3,43,709	4,53,414 (10.6)	5,11,079 (12.7)	6,16,747 (20.7)	6,92,350 (12.3)
(i) Tax Receipts	2,74,974	3,58,224 (10.1)	4,09,588 (14.3)	4,89,098 (19.4)	5,72,979 (17.2)
(ii) Non-tax receipts	68,735	95,191 (12.8)	1,01,491 (6.6)	1,27,649 (25.8)	1,19,371 (-6.5)
B. Non-debt capital receipts	7,629	16,067 (36.9)	43,259 (169.2)	17,973 (-58.5)	7,629 (-57.6)
II Total disbursements	5,40,423	7,27,151 (11.5)	8,45,338 (16.3)	9,46,132 (11.9)	9,91,960 (4.8)
A. Developmental	2,74,483	3,59,331 (10.3)	4,11,815 (14.6)	4,63,722 (12.6)	4,94,238 (6.6)
B. Non-developmental	2,57,142	3,39,086 (10.6)	3,68,474 (8.7)	4,21,112 (14.3)	4,64,810 (10.4)
(i) Revenue	2,39,294	3,21,920 (11.5)	3,49,492 (8.6)	3,80,031 (8.7)	4,18,740 (10.2)
(ii) Interest payments	1,10,451	1,58,624 (14.5)	1,76,570 (11.3)	1,88,540 (6.8)	2,08,171 (10.4)
C. Others	8,798	28,734 (75.5)	65,046 (126.4)	61,298 (-5.8)	32,913 (-46.3)
(i) Revenue	4,539	6,052 (11.1)	6,898 (14.0)	7,969 (15.5)	8,804 (10.5)
(ii) Capital	4,259	22,682 (144.2)	58,148 (156.4)	53,329 (-8.3)	24,109 (-54.8)

Note: Figures in brackets are percentage changes over the previous years.

The revenue deficit accounted for Rs. 1,21,393 crore has increased to Rs. 1,59,350 crore (31.3%) between 1999-00 and 2001-02. It has declined to Rs. 1,28,356 crores in 2004-05 (19.5%) and estimated in 2005-06 budget at Rs. 1,19,806 crore (6.7%). The combined Gross Fiscal Deficit (GFD) as percentage of Gross Domestic Product (GDP) shows gradual decline over the years and estimated at 7.7 per cent in 2005-06 budget estimate from that of the earlier high figures of 10 per cent in 2001-02, and 9.5 per cent of 2002-03. The total disbursements estimated at 28.5 per cent less than that of the proportion of the previous two years (30.6 per cent and 30.5 per cent). The same trend can be seen in the case of total receipts at 28.6 per cent (30.7 and 30.3 per cents respectively in the previous two years).

Deficit indicators of State Governments. A notable feature of the consolidated fiscal position of the State Governments during 2002-03 was the reduction in revenue deficit or in government dis-savings. There are surpluses of Primary revenue balances in all the post-reform years except in 2000-01. As a reform measure, a sustained correction can be seen in the primary deficit as proportion to GDP in all the succeeding years except in 2003-04. The primary revenue balance financed over 21 per cent of interest payments during 2002-03 as against around 5 per cent in 2001-02. It is expected to cover 50.4 and 73.5 per cent in 2004-05 and 2005-06 respectively indicating the impact of fiscal reform measures. (Table 3). The reduction in the revenue deficit in the recent years is on account of higher realisation of states' own tax revenue, especially sales tax revenue as well as increases in the States' share in Central Tax revenue

Table 3
Major deficit Indicators of States–1990-91 to 2005-06

Item	*1990-95 average*	*1995-00 average*	*2000-01 accounts*	*2001-02 accounts*	*2002-03 accounts*	*2003-04*	*2004-05 (RE)*	*2005-06 (BE)*
1	2	3	5	6	7	8	9	10
Gross Fiscal Deficit	21374 (2.8)	55722 (3.5)	89,532 (4.3)	95,994 (4.2)	1,02,123 (4.1)	1,21,420 (4.8)	1,19,288 (4.2)	1,07,041 (3.5)
Revenue Deficit	5209 (0.7)	27617 (1.7)	53,569 (2.6)	59,188 (2.6)	55,111 (2.2)	61,238 (2.4)	43,190 (1.5)	24,494 (0.8)
Primary Deficit	7770 (1.6)	23989 (1.4)	37,830 (1.8)	33,488 (1.5)	31,981 (1.3)	40,660 (1.6)	32,142 (1.1)	14,666 (0.5)
Primary Revenue Balance	- 8395 (-1.0)	-4116 (-0.4)	1867 (0.1)	-3318 (-0.1)	-15031 (-0.6)	-19,522 (-0.8)	-43,956 (1.6)	-67,881 (-2.2)

* (-): Indicates surplus.

• Figures in brackets are percentage to GDP.

The ratio of GFD/GDP of all the States which was 2.6 per cent in 1995-96 increased year after year and reached to 4.7 per cent in 1999-00. Revenue deficit and primary deficit also maintained a similar trend. The States were confronted with growing interest burden, increasing pension liabilities, large administrative expenditure, losses incurred by state public sector undertakings inappropriate user charges and deceleration in current transfers. The fiscal stress, in turn had seriously affected the ability to discharge their basic responsibility of developing social and economic infrastructure.

RECEIPTS OF THE STATE GOVERNMENTS

The total receipts as a ratio to GDP shows improvement over the post reform years. The receipts which was 16.0 in 1990 has reached at 20.5 in 2003-04, but estimated at 18.7 only in 2005-06, per haps the outturn of Value Added Tax (VAT) in lieu of Sales Tax is under observation. Not withstanding the fact that the TR/GDP ratio is favourable, the percentage increase over the years shows fluctuations. Both States' own tax revenue and share in Central Taxes shows the maximum growth in 2004-05 over the Previous years. (Table 4). The non-tax receipts including the grants from the Centre continued to be lower in several years and does not show any uniform growth or impact. The share of own tax revenue to total revenue receipts of all states ranged between 59 per cent and 61 per cent during 2000-01 and 2003-04. The average annual growth rate from 1995-96 to 2004-05 is 11.6 in States own tax revenue 10.8 in the case of total revenue and 11.0 in the share of central taxes and grants. A comparative trend of selected states (Table 5) indicates variations in different states. The per capita states own tax revenue of Rs. 367 has increased to Rs. 1559 between 1990-91 and 2003-04. The index of states own taxes during the period shows wide fluctuations between the different states ranging from 310 to 1172 in Bihar and Punjab respectively (Table 6)

EXPENDITURE OF THE STATE GOVERNMENTS:

The revenue expenditure of the States during 1990-91 of Rs. 67860 crore has increased by 82.4 per cent in 1994-95.

Between 1995-96 and 2000-01 the rise accounts for 93.6 per cent and estimated to increase by 52.9 per cent between 2005-06 and 2000-01.

Table 4
Receipts of the State Governments–1990-91 to 2005-06

Item	*1990-91*	*2000-01*	*2002-03*	*2003-04*	*2004-05 (RE)*	*2005-06 (RE)*
Total Receipts	91160 (16.0) 19.0	349544 (16.7) 12.5	425073 (17.3) 13.7	517563 (20.5) 21.8	578069 (20.4) 11.7	570479 (18.7) -1.3
A. Revenue Receipts	66467 (11.7) 17.6	237953 (11.4) 14.8	280339 (11.4) 9.6	309230 (12.3) 10.3	377132 (13.3) 22.0	421342 (13.8) 11.7
1. Tax Receipts	44586 (7.8) 14.1	168715 (8.10) 15.0	198798 (8.1) 10.3	222606 (8.8) 12.0	263294 (9.3) 18.3	299513 (9.8) 13.8
States Own Tax Revenue	30344 (5.3) 16.7	117981 (5.6) 15.0	142143 (5.8) 11.0	157691 (6.3) 10.9	185494 (6.6) 17.6	212353 (7.0) 14.5
Share in Central Taxes	14242 (2.8) 8.7	50734 (2.7) 15.0	56655 (2.5) 8.5	64915 (2.6) 14.6	77800 (2.7) 19.8	87160 (2.9) 12.0
2. Non-Tax Receipts	21881 (3.8) 25.5	69238 (3.3) 14.4	81541 (3.3) 8.2	86624 (3.4) 6.2	113838 (4.0) 31.4	121811 (4.0) 7.0
Interest Receipts	2403 (0.4) -8.8	11438 (0.5) 93.1	9501 (0.4) 3.2	8564 (0.3) -9.9	11738 (0.4) 37.1	8210 (0.3) -30.1
B. Capital Receipts	24693 (4.3) 22.9	111591 (5.3) 7.7	144734 (5.9) 22.4	208333 (8.3) 43.9	200937 (7.1) -3.6	149155 (4.9) -25.8
Recovery of Loans and Advances	1501 (0.3) 44.6	6898 (0.3) 105.2	3905 (0.2) -49.7	16402 (0.7) 320	9653 (0.3) -41.1	5495 (0.2) -43.1

Note: Figures in brackets are percentages to GDP.
Figures in Italics are Percentage change over the previous year.

The capital expenditure grew by 20.4 per cent per annum on an average. Between 1995-96 and 1999-2000 the percentage growth is only 12.5 per cent. The budgeted estimate for 2005-06 is an increase of 23.8 per cent. The total expenditure which accounted for Rs. 91088 in 1990-91 has increased to Rs. 1777584

Table 5
Tax Revenues of States–Comparison
(Percentage to total revenue)

Sl. No.	*States*	*1999-00*		*2000-01*		*2002-03*		*2003-04*	
		States' own tax	*Share in central taxes*	*States' own tax*	*Share in central taxes*	*States' own tax*	*Share in central taxes*	*States' own tax*	*Share in central taxes*
1.	Andhra Pradesh	61	23	61	23	67	15	68	13
2.	Bihar	35	49	28	64	28	58	30	57
3.	Gujarat	64	13	65	11	62	10	62	9
4.	Karnataka	67	19	68	19	73	16	73	15
5.	Kerala	72	21	72	20	75	15	76	15
6.	Maharashtra	73	11	70	10	76	8	74	8
7.	Punjab	57	9	57	8	56	5	53	5
8.	Tamil Nadu	73	18	73	17	76	15	76	15
9.	West Bengal	59	34	52	37	55	31	58	30
10.	All States	58	25	59	25	61	20	61	19

Table 6
Per Capita States Own Tax Revenue–Comparison
(in Rupees)

Sl. No.	*States*	*1990-91*	*1999-00*	*2001-02*	*2003-04*	*Index of 2003-04 over 1990-91*
1.	Andhra Pradesh	417	1201	1659	2069	496
2.	Bihar	134	369	295	415	310
3.	Gujarat	591	1708	1828	1919	325
4.	Karnataka	521	1499	1868	2315	444
5.	Kerala	450	1618	1860	2678	595
6.	Maharashtra	686	1906	2200	2578	377
7.	Punjab	215	1687	1985	2519	1172
8.	Tamil Nadu	277	1776	2095	2497	901
9.	West Bengal	235	651	811	1052	448
10.	All States	367	1039	1221	1559	425

in 1995-96 and in between 1999-2000 to 2005-06 there is an increase of Rs. 253946 crore with an annual average increase of 13.5 per cent only. The developmental expenditure during 1990-95 (average) accounted for 67.1 per cent of the total expenditure and non-developmental expenditure to the extent of 27.6 per cent. It has reached to the level of 52.6 per cent and 32.6 per cents respectively; much less than the proportion of 1995-00 (73.6 per cent and 38.2 per cent respectively). The three major items of non-developmental expenditure viz interest payments, administrative services (salaries) and pensions together accounted for 23.9 per cent of the total expenditure during 1990-95 (average). It has further increased to 32.9 per cent during 1995-00. The Budget Estimate for 2005-06 accounts for 32.8 per cent (Table 7).

Table 7
Expenditure Pattern of State Governments
(Rs. in crore)

Item	*1990 -95 average*	*1995- 00 average*	*2000- 01*	*2001- 02*	*2002- 03*	*2003- 04*	*2004- 05*	*2005- 06*
I Total Expenditure	122911	202231 (12.9)	347199 (10.6)	377312 (8.7)	420462 (11.4)	516350 (22.8)	584073 (13.1)	567835 (-2.8)
II Development Expenditure	82452 67.1	148779 (16.1) 73.6	210543 (12.4) 60.6	216696 (2.9) 57.4	228417 (5.4) 54.3	274080 (20.0) 53.1	307425 (12.2) 52.6	316793 (3.1) 55.8
i. Economic Services	44086 35.9	71202 (12.3) 35.2	96853 (14.9) 27.9	99736 (3.0) 26.4	105918 (6.2) 25.2	143945 (35.9) 27.9	153868 (6.9) 26.3	149367 (-2.9) 26.3
ii. Social Services	38366 31.2	77577 (20.4) 38.4	113690 (10.4) 32.7	116961 (2.9) 31.0	122499 (4.7) 29.1	130136 (6.2) 25.2	153557 (18.0) 26.3	167425 (9.0) 29.5
III Non-developmental	33885 27.6	77184 (25.6) 38.2	118887 (7.9) 34.2	138080 (16.1) 36.6	151898 (10.0) 36.1	166074 (9.3) 32.2	190679 (14.8) 32.6	208264 (9.2) 36.7
i. Interest payments	13605 11.1	31733 (26.6) 15.7	51702 (14.5) 14.9	62506 (20.9) 16.6	70142 (12.2) 16.7	80760 (15.1) 15.6	87147 (7.9) 14.9	92375 (6.0) 16.3
ii. Administrative services	9262 7.5	17752 (18.3) 8.8	25399 (7.7) 7.3	26894 (5.9) 7.1	27371 (1.8) 6.5	27983 (2.2) 5.4	31626 (13.0) 5.4	39814 (25.9) 7.0
iii. Pension etc.	6454 5.3	16950 (32.5) 8.4	28484 (13.6) 8.2	32753 (15.0) 8.7	36563 (11.6) 8.7	38217 (4.5) 7.4	45394 (18.8) 7.8	54063 (19.1) 9.5

Note: Figures in brackets are percentage changes over the previous years. Figures in Italics are percentages of total expenditure.

The percapita development expenditure of all states in India which was Rs. 689 in 1999-00 has increased to Rs. 1690 in 2000-01 and to 1917 in 2003-04. The expenditure of Gujarat, Karnataka, Maharashtra, Punjab and Tamil Nadu are above the all states level. In Kerala it is only Rs. 673 during 1999-00. During 2003-04 this accounted for Rs. 2743 in much above the all Sates average of Rs. 1917 (Table 8). The percapita expenditure on non-developmental item has increased by more than five fold between 1999-00 and 2003-04 at all States level and in Kerala the similar trend can be observed. In Punjab the increase is more than seven fold. (Table 9).

Table 8
Per Capita Development Expenditure of States (Revenue Account)

(In Rupees)

Sl. No.	*States*	*1999-00*	*2000-01*	*2002-03*	*2003-04*
1.	Andhra Pradesh	683	1904	2085	2420
2.	Bihar	419	813	835	858
3.	Gujarat	908	3284	2862	2874
4.	Karnataka	755	2020	2297	2363
5.	Kerala	673	1973	2264	2743
6.	Maharashtra	779	2415	2199	2041
7.	Punjab	1561	2164	2494	2936
8.	Tamil Nadu	1207	2011	2338	2078
9.	West Bengal	497	1540	1425	1404
10.	All India	689	1690	1849	1917

Table 9
Per Capita Expenditure on Non-development Services

(In Rupees)

Sl. No.	*States*	*1999-00*	*2000-01*	*2002-03*	*2003-04*
1.	Andhra Pradesh	238	1131	1437	1591
2.	Bihar	205	622	865	906
3.	Gujarat	293	1274	1644	1681
4.	Karnataka	262	1081	1402	1543
5.	Kerala	332	1691	1870	1974
6.	Maharashtra	348	1614	1950	2142
7.	Punjab	434	2775	3699	3624
8.	Tamil Nadu	260	1352	1651	1852
9.	West Bengal	237	1229	1632	1829
10.	All India	268	1184	1514	1656

The pecapita expenditure on education, medical and public health shows wide variations across the States. Between 1999-00 and 2003-04 the percapita expenditure on education has increased from Rs. 190 to Rs. 673. In the case of medical and public health the increase is from Rs. 59 to 162 (Table 10). The percapita expenditure on social services during the period increased from Rs. 974 to Rs. 1205 only. Kerala shows the maximum amount on this head among other major States, where the increase is well above the all States level. (Table 11).

Table 10
Per Capita Expenditure on Education, Medical and Public Health

(in Rupees)

Sl. No.	States	1990-91		1999-00		2001-02		2003-04	
		Education	Health	Education	Health	Education	Health	Education	Health
1.	Andhra Pradesh	171	52	442	124	511	145	661	157
2.	Bihar	142	39	427	77	371	65	438	69
3.	Gujarat	226	61	714	173	645	127	731	149
4.	Karnataka	187	62	583	158	665	164	734	165
5.	Kerala	269	90	818	189	782	205	911	236
6.	Maharashtra	222	68	806	142	970	169	854	184
7.	Punjab	281	91	775	219	755	238	917	262
8.	Tamil Nadu	201	66	717	167	692	161	803	196
9.	West Bengal	218	73	639	147	567	155	579	166
10.	All States	190	59	571	131	593	138	673	162

As part of the Institutional Reforms, State Governments viz. Karnataka, Kerala, Tamil Nadu, Punjab and Uttar Pradesh have already enacted Fiscal Responsibility Legislation (FRL) and formulated Medium Term Fiscal Plan to bring about an orderly correction of their financial position. On power sector reforms, the States have constituted State Electricity Regulatory Commissions for determining the tariff structure, unbundling of State Electricity Boards into separate entities of Power generation, transmission and distribution, raising power tariffs and measures for reducing transmission and distribution losses. Setting up of Special Economic Zones (SEZ) and Agro Export

Zones are other major measures initiated to boost infrastructure.

Table 11
Per Capita Expenditure on Social and Economic Services
(In Rupees)

Sl. No.	States	1999-00		2000-01		2002-03		2003-04	
		Social dev. services	*Econo-mics services*	*Social dev. services*	*Econo-mics services*	*Social dev. services*	*Econo-mics services*	*Social dev. services*	*Econo-mics services*
1.	Andhra Pradesh	978	513	1065	840	1188	897	1373	1047
2.	Bihar	631	311	583	230	570	265	629	229
3.	Gujarat	1303	1148	1599	1685	1436	1426	1534	1341
4.	Karnataka	1060	775	1177	842	1217	1081	1313	1049
5.	Kerala	1310	718	1298	675	1413	851	1606	1136
6.	Maharashtra	1235	581	1575	840	934	624	990	539
7.	Punjab	1161	789	1272	892	1522	972	1519	1417
8.	Tamil Nadu	1243	702	1261	749	1347	991	1463	615
9.	West Bengal	1045	386	1065	475	1022	403	1011	393
10.	All States	974	559	1048	642	1147	702	1205	713

DEBT OUTSTANDING

The public debt of the State Governments comprises of internal debt, small savings, provident fund and loans and advances from Government of India. The debt outstanding of the States shows an increase of more than six fold during 1990-91 and 2004-05 (Table 12) i.e. from Rs. 108203 crore to Rs. 791400 crore. In the case of Kerala it accounts for about seven fold. The rising debt of the State Governments is a reflection of the deterioration in the fiscal performance and signifies long term mismatch between the growth of revenue and expenditure of the States. The per capita debt at all States level has increased from Rs. 2543 to Rs. 6531 during 1997 and 2003. In the case of Kerala the per capita debt accounts for Rs. 3630 and Rs. 9248 which is the highest among all States.Based on the recommendation of Eleventh Finance Commission, the Government of India setup an Incentive Fund to encourage State Governments to initiate fiscal reforms. Releases from the Incentive Fund were based on a single monitorable fiscal objective viz. a minimum improvement of 5 percentage points in the ratio of revenue deficit to revenue receipts in each year till 2004-2005 over the base year 1999-2000. The Debt Swap Scheme introduced by the Central Government (2003-04) would enable States to prepay their high cost debt to the Centre through additional market borrowings and proceeds from small savings at the prevailing interest rates, over a period of three years ending 2004-05. Of the total outstanding high cost loans amounting to Rs. 114317 crore as at the end of March 2002, Rs. 92369 crore ie. 80.8% small savings loans and Rs. 50404 crore of market loans has been swapped so far. The balance to be swapped is only Rs. 21948 crore. DSS would be extended by allowing States to raise fresh loans and repay their old high cost loans to NABARD and some other agencies. States were permitted to increase their open market borrowings and reduce their dependence on loans from the Centre.

Table 12
Debt Outstanding-States

(Rupees in crore)

Sl. No.	*States*	*1991*	*2000*	*2002*	*2003*	*2004*
1.	Andhra Pradesh	6743	29114	42492	50377	57574
2.	Bihar	9231	28353	39324	44875	49882
3.	Gujarat	6230	22984	36938	46771	55318
4.	Karnataka	4633	18725	27166	32021	38091
5.	Kerala	4442	20176	26951	29987	33708
6.	Maharashtra	9850	38300	52795	63543	71759
7.	Punjab	6859	23662	32496	37060	42057
8.	Tamil Nadu	5501	23839	32691	39753	44834
9.	West Bengal	7870	37006	58275	69241	79575
10.	All India	108203	420135	586687	688421	791400

Between 2002-04, the State of Kerala alone swapped nearly Rs. 1000 crore of high cost debt. The Reserve Bank of India has been providing Ways and Means Advances (WMA) and overdraft facility to the State Governments. The consolidated Sinking Fund envisages redumption of market loans. The States, Maharashtra and Kerala have been permitted to raise upto 50 per cent of their allocation through auction in 2002-03.

Kerala accessed the Ways and Means Advances on several occasions. Kerala availed WMA on 15 occasions in 2003-04 and on 124 occasions in 2004-05, reflecting the continued short-term pressures on the budgets.

Issues

(i) Gross Fiscal Defict

(ii) Persistant expansion of the revenue deficit

(iii) Large accumulation of debt

(iv) Mounting debt service burden

(v) Rising share of committed but non developmental expenditure

(vi) Low and declining non-tax revenues

(vii) Increasing contingent liabilities

(viii) Poor performance of Public Sector Undertakings

Fiscal consolidation measures proposed in the State budgets explore ways of moderation of expenditure and revenue augmentation. Some states have proposed the setting up of Expenditure Reforms Committees. A few States have identified performance indicators to assess the quality of expenditure restructuring. States have also initiated measures for reduction in non-merit subsidies, better targeting of subsidies and reduction of non-productive expenditures as part of expenditure management.

Many States have announced ways of reducing the cost of administration by proposingt a freeze on fresh recruitment as well as reviewing manpower requirements. The financial health and management of State level Public Sector Undertakings have been a cause for concern in the last few years.

Each State has devised its own measures but most of these have a common thread of reform of public enterprises, reduction in subsidies, expenditure containment and revenue augmentation. There are, however, limitations in regard to the adjustment effort in view of the large magnitude of committed expenditures of which salaries, pensions and interest charges are crucial.

CONCLUSION

Economic reform in a broader sense would also encompass realigning of relative functions of centre and State towards achieving economic prosperity and improving the quality of life. In our country, states are of varying sizes and are at different levels of economic and social development. Many States are larger in terms of population. Some states have progressed very well interms of social development and many States have also done well in rapid economic development. Individually, some states are world-class performers in some respects especially on social sectors. However, the two most important areas of concern are social infrastructure which includes primary education, primary health, social security and to some extent law and order. Physical infrastructure emphasis water supply (both for drinking and irrigation), drainage, roads, power supply, medium and minor ports etc. Both of these are in the State's domain. Thus expenditure responsibility of States is likely to grow in social sectors. Therefore Economic Reform is not sustainable if expenditure of State Governments is not brought in desired directions.

Note: All the data used in the tables are compiled from websites of Reserve Bank of India, Central Statistical Organisation, Government of India, Ministry of Finance, Government of Kerala and various issues of RBI Bulletins.

REFERENCES

Favaro and Lahiri (eds) (2003), *Fiscal Policies and sustainable Growth in India*, Oxford University Press, New Delhi.

Reddy, Y.V. (2000), *"Fiscal Reforms at State-Level: Review and Prospects"*, (speech Delivered at India States' Reform Forum Organised by the World Bank, at New Delhi, November 2000).

Rangarajan, C. (2004), *"Economic Reforms: Same Issues and Concerns for the 21st Century"* (Speech Delivered at the Annual Conference of the Indian Economic Association at Vellore, 2004).

Raja, J. Chelliah (2005), *"The Malady of continuing fascal imbalance : The impossible Quadrangle"*. The Fourth Ambirajan Memorial Lecture (16, Feb. 2005).

Central Statistical Organisation website.

Handbook of Statistics on State Government Finances (RBI website).

Govt. of India, Indian Public Finance Statistics, Ministry of Finance, Various Issues.

RBI State Finances: A Study of Budgets (Various Years) RBI website

Website : http: india budget.nic.in

Kerala gov. in budget 2005-06/budget brief.htm.

Govt. of Kerala, Economic Review 2004 and 2005, State Planning Board, Trivandrum.

P.S. MOHANAKUMAR

External Sector and Economic Reforms in India

6

India's external sector reforms record a success story viewed from macroeconomic ankle. But it points a dismal picture since reforms failed to cultivate complementarily between growth and social opportunity even though many claim that post-reform experience could reduce poverty. But Least Developed Countries 2004 report assesses no positive relationship between international trade and poverty alleviation. The reason can be attributed to weaker linkages between trade and economic growth in developing countries. The export expansion path created led to an exclusive form of economic growth. (Enclave-led growth). The endogenous growth theory (New growth theory) calls for knowledge and technological spill over in developing countries as a result of capital flows. This normally translates into a higher growth rate for the economy. The famous Kuznet-Denison–Solow growth model also account constant returns to scale production function with both domestic and foreign capital. One can view the relationship between growth and openness both from academic and social point of new. Many studies are available to link growth and development to that of capital flows and openness.

Theoretically, endogenous theory of growth gives credentials to relate 'openness' and 'growth'. This is via capital flows, innovation, technology transfer, technological and knowledge spill over. There are strong theoretical grounds that trade promotes growth and that growth leads to increasing income and improved standard of living of the poor. Growth may be export-oriented as in the case of India where the benefits are transferred to the trading partners, in many cases. As Bhagavati puts it, it can be immiserising when world markets are excessively competitive. If one reviews past studies there are situations where openess lead to economic growth, and at the same time the opposite relations were established in quite other cases. The reasons for positive relationship are due to the strong absorptive capacity of the country and the impact of capital flows depends upon varying location-specific factors. These location specific factors are invariably absent in "immature economics" like India than in "mature economies". Mature economies denote to a situation of well developed markets with strong regulatory and institutional framework.In India, many studies suggest that liberalization has not contributed significantly towards economic growth or productivity. The New Economic Policy (NEP) of 1990-91 ushered a new era in the country whereby many external sector variables show positive signs. But there is no room for full satisfaction since we are facing very serious challenges because of widening inequality, rising unemployment problems and increased poverty. (There exists controversy about Indian poverty statistics). There is little reason to celebrate reform process due to a rising rural-urban income gap. In India the ratio of the income of a lowest worker to that of top executives remains as 1: 30000. This is true wherever market economy is practiced. In USA since 1973 the average income of the top 1% of has doubled and the income of the top 0.1% has tripled. In developing countries the things are much worse. Some of the available statistics help one to diagonise the present situation and correct the misalignment. If globalization is viewed from the point cf view of text book definition-i.e. Trade, capital flows, international movement of workers and technological flows– it works well in India, and from the human ankle (social returns)–poverty, health, unemployment, equality-it acts as a boomerang. A few important variables with regard to the performance of Indian Economy for a ten year period begins from 1990-91 are given below.

	1990-91	2001-02
FDI	$129 million	$3904 million
Portfolio	$4 million	$2021 million
Total (FDI +Portfolio+ NRI+GDR+FII)	$133 million	$5925 million
Forex	$1 billion	$102billion
External Dept.	–	$101.13 billion
Debt. GDP ratio	38.7%	22.1%
Debt service to current receipts	35%	13.8%
Exchange rate (Rs. to US$)	Rs. 17.96	Rs. 48.00 (Rs. 44.00 in 2005)
World Trade Share	0.5%	0.75%
International Competitiveness Ranking	41 (in 1997)	41
GDP per capita ranking	–	106
FDI Confidence Index	–	6 (among 64 countries)
Current account deficit	3.24%	1.2% (Surplus in 2003 & 2004)
Human Development Index (Rank)	–	127
Education Index (Rank)	–	141 (among 173 Countries)
GDP growth rate	1990s	6.0%
GDP growth rate	1980s	5.4%
PCGDP (per capita)	1990s	4.1%
	1980s	3.3%

The external sector during the last decade shows an impressive performance in terms of some of the macro indicators shown above. Indian economy has acquired considerable strength due to the globalization process initiated during the beginning of 1990s. The post-reform experience did not contribute much to reduce the poverty and opposite casual claims were done by economists to prove the disastrous effect of globalization, supported by facts and evidences. Even though the exports increased during the last few years, the export-led growth may probably be proved to be immiserising since much of the benefit is exported away. Also there is a notion that GDP growth will enhance the well being of the people due to trickle down effects and reduced unemployment rate. The relationship between reduction in unemployment and GDP growth was proved by Arthur Okun (Okun's law), which states specifically that changes in unemployment rate between two periods of time will be inversely related to the fluctuations of the rate of economic growth around its 'normal rate'. The annual growth rates of employment were 2.04% during 1983-1994 while it decreased to 0.98% during the period 1994-2000. The employment elasticity of GDP was 0.41 in 1983-94 while it decreased to 0.15 in 1994-2000. Compared to many other countries in the world our physical quality index is also very low. While India's literacy rate is only 48% it is 98% in S. Korea, 95% in Thailand and 83% in China. As per the international poverty line (US$ 1 per day) 44% of the people in India are still below the poverty line. Even though the number of BPL people in India is only 26% as per the Planning Commission official estimate, but it is much above 40% as per alternate estimates.

The financial services sector alone recorded a growth rate during the period while the manufacturing and agricultural sector recorded a poor growth rate. The removal of restriction, and protection adversely affected the small scale sector in India. Trade doesn't act as an engine of growth to small manufacturing enterprises. New intervention strategies such as cluster based approaches have not been very successful in India. In the health care sector also India was not able to implement the Bhore Committee report of 1948 by ensuring health care to all through the states. The health sector reforms in 1990s derived a new concept equal to that of the capacity to pay to a 'commodity' with the prevailing ideology of market. Bhore Committee suggests 15% of budgetary allocation for health while in India it is less than one fourth of 15%. The number of low birth-weight babies is 33 per thousand in India while it is 6 in china, 9 in S. Korea, 6 in Thailand 8 in Indonesia and 25 in Pakistan. In India more than 50% of the children are under nourished and 80% of the pregnant women suffer from malnutrition. The ultimate aim of any reform package is upliftment of the poor. Liberalization has failed to achieve this basic objective. One has to view liberalization in terms of the Millennium Development Goals set by the UN.

1. Poverty reduction
2. Education to all
3. Ensuring proper health care
4. Employment generation

One has to link liberalization to capital flows with that of economic growth, poverty reduction and employment opportunities. As Grossman and Helpman rightly put it, transfer of technology, through FDI flows could impact R&D of developing countries in that they could stimulate innovation thereby enhancing growth in the host country. It creates knowledge and technological "spillovers" on economic growth. The review of select studies does not give much reliable information regarding the positive relationship between liberalization and economic growth due to knowledge and technological spillovers. It may be because we failed to manage globalization in the right perspective or India may not be matured enough to gauge the benefits in full and translate the benefits it into the poorer sections of the society. We failed to cultivate an effective complementarity between growth and social opportunity. In India the working families are not getting due share of economic growth and hence face growing insecurity. As Krugman rightly puts it "Politicians are systematically making things worse". 65% of the people in India do not have a bank account while the figure is 75% among rural house holds. In India, poor people and lower middle class are at the receiving end and the government does not even assure 'minimum procurement price" for the products of the farming community. Even after a decade of reforms, 10 millions farmers live and die in debt. Suicide by farmers and starvation deaths are reported from many states in India. This situation can be attributed to the weak linkage between trade and economic growth. Review of some of the studies may help to verify these facts for reaching valid conclusions about Indian situation.

The studies which examined the relationship of openness and economic growth are that of Subrahmanian & et al (1996), Marwah & Klein (1998), Das (2001), Banga (2003) and Mazumdar (2005). All these studies doesn't show a strong positive relationship between growth and openness. The net capital flows (FDI, Portfolio, GDR, FII etc) increased form 2.17% of GDP in 1990-91 to 4.44% of GDP in 1996-97 and to 3.41% of GDP in 2000-01. As per the study (Mazumdar) capital flows have not contributed much to the economic growth or industrial production. Based on the Marwah-Klein (1998) model, out of every 0.35(35%) of growth point generated by both domestic and foreign capital put together, the contribution of FDI and imports together is only 0.087 (9%). Marwah and Klein used the famous Kuznet-Denisan-Solow type growth accounting with constant returns to scale production function with both domestic and foreign capital. The study conducted by Subrahmanian et al also reveals a similar conclusion. There is no significant relationship between capital inflows and export productivity. The performance of foreign firms vis-à-vis domestic firms are also not significantly different.

The studies conducted with regard to other developing countries also replicate similar phenomena. The studies reviewed in their connections are Nunnemkamp *et al.* (2002, 2003, 2005), Rajan (2003), *et al.* and Carkovic Levine (2002). A critical down to earth analysis exposes many facts. The FDI flows represent only 13% of overall capital formation in all lower and middle income countries. Since most of them are commodity related FDI, it fails to provide rising average income or reducing poverty. Capital account liberalization helped only those countries with strong macro economic fundamentals. India was able to avoid a crisis since we retained control over capital account liberalization. Indian began capital account liberalization only in 1993-94, and too with caution. Real Effective Exchange Rate (REER) in India did not depreciate as in the case of East Asia and Latin America. It is an indication of efficient management of capital flows during the ninetees; otherwise it would have led to misalignment. But of late, we are experiencing volatility in exchange rate. The trade balance consequences for Thailand in the 1980s and 1990s were mainly due to the misalignment of Thai Baht. Carkovic-Levine study finds no casual link between FDI and growth. FDI does not have any independent influence on economic growth. It also noticed no positive spillover running from foreign owned to domestic owned firms. The irony was that for over two decades many claim that FDI helps economic growth and technology spill over effects. These studies provide little support for the view that FDI accelerates over all economic growth. China was able to attract more FDI mainly because of its high growth. In the year 2001 total FDI flow in India were US$ 3403 millions while the equivalent figure in China was 46846 million US dollars. A Granger no-casualty test was developed by Toda and Yamamoto (1995) to examine casualty link between FDI growth and real industrial growth for China in the context of FDI led growth hypothesis. There existed a two way casualty running between industrialized growth and FDI growth for China. Economic growth in China for a period of fifteen years from 1980-95 was nearly 10% per annum. Both FDI led growth and growth-driven FDI hypothesis are supported by empirical evidence from China. The belief that growth is led by FDI does not fit well in the case of many African countries and other developing countries. It was growth that attracted FDIs and not FDIs that brought growth. The Sub-Saharan Africa's share of global FDI rose from 0.4 per cent to 0.5 per cent only from 1990 to 2000. The share of overall FDI inflows to developing countries stock is at four per cent.

CONCLUSION

The net results one can draw from these analysis are:

1. FDI related growth depends on strong markets and institutional framework.
2. The correlation between 'openness' and growth are influenced by country specific, location specific factors.
3. Institutions prevailing in poor countries tend to seriously constrain growth-enhancing and poverty alleviating effects of FDI.
4. Suitable policies to avert immiserising growth are not effectively taken/implemented in immature economies. This fails to cultivate complementarities between growth and social opportunity.

If we juxtapose India's external economic indicators with that of the UN millennium development goals viz. poverty reduction, employment generation and economic growth we can safely conclude that there is no strong link between openness and growth and poverty reduction in India. This is also because in Enclave-led growth, the pattern of growth is concentrated in a small part of the economy both geographically and sectorally. Thus the relationship between trade and poverty becomes asymmetrical. The GDP growth rate is not totally related to employment generation. Studies linking these variables are practically absent and theories designed in this respect are also not satisfactory. More research is needed to clearly identify the link between FDI and openness on the one hand and poverty and distribution of income as well as GDP growth on the other hand.

During the post reform period the inequality of economic condition and of opportunity widely increased in India. Inequality in terms of consumption expenditure, in terms of wages, rural–urban disparities in terms of employment have risen sharply. Two indicators related to development and poverty which shows inequality are given below.

- Human development index -: Kerala (0.59), Bihar (0.31)
- Human poverty index -: Kerala (20), Bihar (52)

The per capita consumption expenditure in India after 1991 decreased in Bihar, Orissa, Assam, Tamil Nadu, Haryana, Karnataka, Gujarat, Rajasthan, Himachal Pradesh, and Punjab while it increased only in Kerala, U.P, M.P, Maharashtra. There are no definite studies to link trade and consumption in India. In virtuous trade effect, the average private consumption per capita will rise (per capita consumption increased only in 4 states). In India the effect of trade is immiserizing since average private consumption per capita in many states decreased even after a decade of liberalized trade.

REFERENCES

Banga, Rashmi (2003), "The Differential Impact of Japanese and US, FDI on Exports of Indian Manufacturing ICRIER Working paper.

Carkovic, Maria & Ross Levine (2002), "Does Foreign Direct Investment Accelerate Economic Growth", University of Minnesota Working paper NBER, Cambridge.

Das, Deb Kusum (2003), "Quantifying Trade Business: Has Protection Declined Substantially in Indian Manufacturing" ICRIER Working paper.

Mazumder, Tanushree (2005), "Capital Flows into India, Implications for its Economic Growth" *Economic and Political Weekly,* May 21, 2005.

Nunnen Kamp, Peter (2002), "To What Extent FDI Help Achieve International Development Goals" Keil Institute of World Economics, Working paper 1128.

Nunnen Kamp, Peter (2002), "Determinants of FDI in Developing Countries: has Globalization Changes the Rule of Game." Keil Institute of World Economics, Working paper 1122.

Nunnen Kamp, Peter (2002), "Why Economic Growth Trade Differ so much Across Developing Countries. The Globalization Debate and its Relevance to Pakistan" Keil Institute of World Economics, Working paper 1091.

Nunnen Kamp, Peter and Julius Spatze (2003), FDI and Economic Growth in Developing Countries: How Relevant are Host Country and Industry Characteristics, Keil Institute of World Economics, Working paper 1176.

Nunnen Kamp, Peter and Foulker (2005), "Do, Multinational Enterprises Contribute to Convergence or Divergence? A Disaggregated Analysis of US FDI" Keil Institute of World Economics, Working paper 1242.

Rajan, Ramakrishnan, Rahul Sen and Reza Sireger "Misalignment of the Bath and its Trade Balance Consequences for Thailand in the 1980s". *The World Economy,* 26(a), 2003, pp. 1325-56.

Shan, Jordan, Gary Tain & Fiona San (1997), The FDI led Growth Hypothesis: Further Econometric Evidence from China. Economics Division Working paper, National Centre for Development Studies, Australia.

Subramaniam, K.K. *et al.* (1996), "Foreign Collaboration Under Liberalization Policy: Patterns of FDI and Technology-Transfer in Indian Industry Since 1991" RBI Study.

PART - V
Economic Growth, Poverty and Public Distribution System

K. RAJAN

Growth and Inequality in India During the Post Reform Period

7

INTRODUCTION

The ultimate aim of Economic Reforms in India was the betterment of living conditions of the people especially of the poor. Hence reforms aimed acceleration of the low economic growth of the country, which is considered to be the root cause of high incidence of poverty. The new measures will have varied effects on the economy in general and on economic growth, inter-state disparities in growth and inequality in particular. There are divergent views among economists regarding the impact of reforms. The supporters of reforms argue that economic reforms will result in higher economic growth and reduction in inequality and will improve the living conditions of the people in general. On the other hand, critics of reforms argue that reforms will result in large scale unemployment, higher inequality and poverty and worsening the living conditions of the majority of people in India. In this context, the present paper is an attempt to examine the impact of reforms on economic growth, disparities in economic growth across Indian states and on inequality in India. The specific objectives of the paper are:

OBJECTIVES OF THE PAPER

The major objectives of the paper are:

1. To examine the economic growth of India during the post reform period.
2. To analyse the inter-state disparities in economic growth in India during the post reform period and;

3. To examine the inequality in India during the post reform period.

The paper is based on secondary data from published sources and it is divided into V sections. Section I contains an introduction and objectives of the paper. Section II examines economic growth of India during the post reform period. Inequality in the growth rates across the states in India is examined in Section III. Section IV examines the post reform trends in inequality in terms of consumption. The major findings are summarised in the last section.

SECTION - II

Economic Reforms and Economic Growth

One of the important objectives of Economic Planning in India has been rapid Economic growth. Hence, efforts were made to accelerate the growth rate of the economy by all available means during the plan period. However, the rate of growth achieved in India was quite low till 1980s. It was in this context that the government of India adopted economic reforms to accelerate economic growth so as to reduce the high incidence of poverty, which was believed to be the result of low economic growth. It is generally agreed that economic growth that spreads its benefits equitably among the population is helpful in reducing poverty. In this section, we have examined the growth rate of the Indian economy during the post reform period of 1990-91 to 2004-05 in terms of annual growth rates in Gross National Product (GNP FC), Net National Product (NNP FC), Per capita Net National Product (PNNP FC) and Real Gross Domestic Product (GDP FC). Table 1 gives an account of the growth performance of Indian economy during the post reform period.

According to the table, there are considerable variations in the growth rate in India during the post reform period. The annual growth rate of Indian economy in terms of GNP FC was more than 5 per cent for the years from 1990-91 to 1996-97, except for the year 1991-92. It is more than 7 per cent for the years 1994-95 and 1995-96 and it is even more than 8 per cent for the year 1996-97. The growth rate is more than 4 per cent per annum for the years from 1997-98 to 2003-04 while it is more than 6 per cent for the years 1998-99, 1999-2000, 2001-02 and it is even more than 8 per cent for the year 2003-04.

Table 1
Annual Growth Rate of GNP, NNP, PGDP During the Post Reform Period

Base 1993-94 — Per cent

Year	*GNP FC*	*NNP FC*	*Per capita NNP FC*	*Real GDP FC (Industry Origin)*
1990-91	5.5	5.4	3.3	5.6
1991-92	1.1	0.5	-1.5	1.3
1992-93	5.1	5.0	3.1	5.1
1993-94	5.9	5.8	3.4	5.9
1994-95	7.2	7.1	4.9	7.3
1995-96	7.5	7.3	5.2	7.3
1996-97	8.2	8.2	6.1	7.8
1997-98	4.9	4.6	2.6	4.8
1998-99	6.4	6.5	4.4	6.5
1999-00	6.2	6.3	4.4	6.1
2000-01	4.3	4.2	2.3	4.4
2001-02	6.0	6.2	4.3	5.8
2002-03 P	4.2	4.2	2.4	4.0
2003-04 Q	8.5	9.0	7.1	8.5

Source: Economic Survey (2004-05), Government of India, P-S4.
P-Provisional, Q-Quick estimate

The annual growth rate of NNP FC is more than 5 per cent for the period 1990-91 to 1993-94, except for the year 1991-92. It is more than 7 per cent for the years 1994-95 and 1995-96 and even more than 8 per cent for the year 1996-97. The annual growth rate of NNP FC is more than 4 per cent for the years 1997-98 to 2003-04 and it is more than 6 per cent for the years 1998-99, 1999-2000 and 2001-02. It is very high (9 per cent) for the year 2003-04.

In terms of per capita NNP FC, it is more than 3 per cent for the years 1990-91, 1992-93 and 1993-94. It is more than 5 per cent in the year 1995-96 and more than 6 per cent for the year 1996-97. It is more than 7 per cent for the year 2003-04.

The annual growth rate of per capita NNP FC is very high (around 5 per cent) for the years 1994-95,1995-96,1996-97 and for the year 2003-04.

The annual growth rate of real GDP FC in India during the post reform period is also very high. It is more than 5 per cent for most of the years and it is more than 7 per cent for the years 1994-95, 1995-96 and 1996-97. It is very much higher (8 per cent) for the year 2003-04.

The above analysis shows that the economic growth of India during the post reform period was very high. Although there are many factors in economic growth, reforms have been one of the most important factors in our very high economic growth. So, it is concluded that reform measures in India are helpful in accelerating economic growth.

SECTION - III

Inter-State Disparities in Economic Growth

The growth performance of India during the post reform period showed that there has been a considerable increase in economic growth in India. However, this does not mean that this higher growth rate of Indian economy during the post reform period is equitably distributed among the Indian states. Economists differ in their opinion regarding interstate disparities in income growth. There are two dominant views and one view is that there will be inter-regional convergence in income growth (there will be a marked reduction in income differentials) and the other is that there will be widening of regional disparities amongst the Indian states (inter-state divergence). Those who supports converge of income with economic development argue that economic reforms will accelerate economic growth and will reduce inequality.

The growth performance of states in India during the post reform period has been examined in terms of GSDP, Per capita GSDP, NSDP, and per capita NSDP. The growth performance of states based on SDP and per capita SDP are presented in table 2. It can be seen that there are considerable variations in the performance of individual states, with some states growing faster than the average and others slower. The range of variation in the growth rate of GSDP across states is from a low of 2.76 per cent per year in Assam to a high of 10.09 per cent per year in Pondicherry.

Table 2
Annual Compound Growth rate in GSDP, Per capita GSDP, NSDP and per capita NSDP of States in India During the Post reform Period (Per cent per annum)
At 1993-94 Prices For 1990-91 to 2000-01

States	*GSDP*	*States*	*Per capita GSDP*	*States*	*NSDP*	*States*	*Per capita NSDP*
Pondicherry	10.09	Pondicherry	8.11	Pondicherry	10.31	Pondicherry	8.34
Goa	8.38	Goa	6.75	Delhi	8.70	Goa	6.97
Sikkim	8.12	Karnataka	5.89	Goa	8.60	Karnataka	5.73
Karnataka	7.56	Tripura	5.60	Sikkim	8.12	Tripura	5.68
Gujarat	7.35	Gujarat	5.56	Karnataka	7.41	Tamil Nadu	5.36
Tripura	7.31	Tamil Nadu	5.52	Tripura	7.40	Sikkim	5.24
West Bengal	6.84	West Bengal	5.10	West Bengal	6.87	West Bengal	5.13
Maharastra	6.83	Sikkim	4.80	Gujarat	6.86	Gujarat	5.07
Delhi	6.83	Maharastra	4.70	Maharastra	6.50	Delhi	4.72
Tamil Nadu	6.62	Kerala	4.58	Manipur	6.49	Kerala	4.56
Manipur	6.33	Himachal Pradesh	4.45	Tamil Nadu	6.46	Maharastra	4.37
Himachal Pradesh	6.31	All-India GDP (CSO)	4.08	A and N Islands	6.13	Himachal Pradesh	4.12
A and N Islands	6.17	Andhra Pradesh	3.92	Himachal Pradesh	5.97	Manipur	4.05
All-India GDP (CSO)	6.10	Manipur	3.91	All-India NDP (CSO)	5.95	Andhra Pradesh	3.88
Rajasthan	6.07	All States GSDP	3.83	Rajasthan	5.95	All States NSDP	3.67
Kerala	5.82	Rajasthan	3.54	Kerala	5.80	All-India NDP (CSO)	3.65
All States GSDP	5.82	Haryana	2.94	Meghalaya	5.78	Rajasthan	3.42
Meghalaya	5.62	Delhi	2.92	All States NSDP	5.65	Haryana	2.76

Contd...

States	*GSDP*	*States*	*Per capita GSDP*	*States*	*NSDP*	*States*	*Per capita NSDP*
Andhra Pradesh	5.44	Punjab	2.89	Andhra Pradesh	5.39	Punjab	2.62
Nagaland	5.28	Madhya Pradesh	2.67	Nagaland	5.27	Madhya Pradesh	2.52
Haryana	5.06	A and N Islands	2.49	Haryana	4.87	A and N Islands	2.41
Punjab	4.85	Orissa	2.28	Madhya Pradesh	4.64	Meghalaya	2.35
Jammu and Kashmir	4.81	Jammu and Kashmir	2.21	Punjab	4.58	Arunachal Pradesh	2.02
Madhya Pradesh	4.78	Meghalaya	2.19	Arunachal Pradesh	4.57	Jammu and Kashmir	1.93
Arunachal Pradesh	4.74	Arunachal Pradesh	2.18	Jammu and Kashmir	4.52	Orissa	1.68
Uttar Pradesh	3.95	Uttar Pradesh	1.86	Uttar Pradesh	3.60	Uttar Pradesh	1.43
Orissa	3.75	Assam	0.93	Orissa	3.14	Nagaland	0.74
Bihar	2.87	Nagaland	0.80	Assam	2.52	Assam	0.69
Assam	2.76	Bihar	0.12	Bihar	2.42	Bihar	-0.31
Coefficient of Variation (percentage)							
For all states	28.14		52.19		32.00		56.39
For 16 major states	27.94		48.02		30.60		53.82

Source: S.L.Shetty, EPW 2003.

The range of variation in per capita GSDP is higher from a low of 0.12 per cent per year in Bihar to 8.11 per cent in Pondicherry. The range of variation in NSDP is between 2.42 per cent in Bihar to 10.31 per cent in Pondicherry whereas the range of variation in per capita NSDP is from –0.31 per cent in Bihar to 8.34 per cent in Pondicherry.

The states are arranged in descending order on the basis of their annual compound growth rates (table 2). The highest annual compound growth rate in GSDP was achieved by Pondicherry (10.9 per cent per annum) followed by Goa (8.38 per cent). The performance of 15 states are higher than the growth of all states GSDP growth rate of 5.82 per cent per annum while 12 states annual compound growth rates are lower than the growth rate of all states. The growth rate of Assam is the lowest (2.76 per cent) followed by Bihar (2.87 per cent). The coefficient of variation for all states is 28.14 per cent whereas it is 27.94 per cent for 16 major states.

In terms of per capita GSDP, Pondicherry and Goa are in the first and second place respectively while the growth rate of per capita GSDP of Bihar is only 0.12 per cent, followed by Nagaland (0.80 per cent), Assam (0.93 per cent). It should be noted that the performance of higher income states like Punjab (2.89 per cent) and Haryana (2.49) are much lower than the growth rate of all states GSDP (3.83 per cent). The coefficient of variation in per capita GSDP for all states was 52.19 per cent whereas it is 48.02 per cent for the 16 major states. However, Kerala's annual growth rate of 4.58 per cent in per capita GSDP is very much higher than the growth rate of 3.80 per cent per annum for all states. On the other hand, Maharastra, which has experienced nearly 6 per cent annual growth in total GSDP could achieve only 4.70 per cent growth rate in terms of per capita SDP.

The performance of states in terms of NSDP also shows that the growth rates of Pondicherry (10.31 per cent), Delhi (8.7 per cent), Goa (8.6 per cent) and Sikkim (8.12 per cent) are much higher than the average growth rate of NSDP for all States (5.65 per cent per annum). However, Bihar (2.42 per cent), Assam (2.52 per cent) Orissa (3.14 per cent) and UP (3.60 per cent) are the states recording lowest growth rates in NSDP. Sixteen states could achieve a higher growth rate of NSDP higher than the growth rate of NSDP for all states while 11 states growth rates are below the average growth rate of all states during the post reform period.

In terms of the per capita NSDP, the performance of Pondicherry and Goa are the best recording 8.34 per cent and 6.97 per cent annual growth rate whereas Bihar recorded a negative growth rate of –0.31 per cent and Assam recorded only 0.69 per cent annual growth rate in per capita NSDP. The per capita NSDP growth rate of 14 states are more than the all states per capita NSDP growth rates while 13 states per capita

NSDP growth rates are below the all states per capita NSDP growth rates. The coefficient of variation for all states in per capita NSDP is 56.39. The coefficient of variation among states in GSDP is 28.14 per cent, per capita GSDP is 52.19 per cent, NSDP is 32.00 per cent and per capita NSDP is 56.39 per cent.

The above analysis of economic growth of Indian states during the post reform period shows that some states are far ahead of others in growth rates. There are significant differences in the growth rates among the Indian states during the post reform period. So reforms have resulted in unequal growth rates and interstate disparities in growth rates. The difference in growth rates is much sharper in terms of per capita SDP and depicts a situation of greater inequality in India during the post reform period. The increased variations in growth performance across states during the post reform period refute the assumption that interstate differences would narrow with development. This can happen if the poorer states actually grow faster than the richest states. However, in India, the growth pattern of the post reform period has resulted in an increase in regional inequality with the poorer states lagging behind in growth.

The growth performance of a region or state depends upon so many factors among which resource endowments, infrastructural development, industrialisation, climate etc are important apart from the state policy. The interstate differences in growth rates may be largely due to the reform policy of the state as some states are able to exploit the new opportunities. The persistently low rate of growth for a group of states in future will result in concentration of poverty in a few states. Hence, it is necessary to increase the rate of growth of those states whose growth rates are very low.

The increasing disparities in income across the states with economic development have serious implications. Hence Planners and policy makers of the government should make sincere efforts to reduce these disparities in economic growth by giving special considerations to those states, which lag behind in economic growth rates so that the states with lower growth rates can improve their performance in future.

SECTION - III

Inequality in India During the Post Reform Period

Inequality of income or expenditure is measured in terms of the percentage of income or expenditure received or spent by the percentage of people in a country. For measuring inequality, there are a large number of methods, of which, Gini Index, Co-efficient of variation, Standard deviation of income power etc. are most commonly used. But ultimately all these measures explain the same thing, inequality. Thus the differences among these measures are one of degree. Lorenz curves are used to represent inequality graphically. A major objective of planned development in India since independence has been to accelerate economic growth and achieve a balanced regional development. The term inequality refers to the unequal distribution of income. A variety of historical, social and political factors, interact with economic factors in determining ones income and differences in income are on account of differences in individuals talent, acquired training and skills, occupation, experience and inherited property.

In India, there is widespread inequality in the distribution of income, and the degree of inequality has been on increase inspite of our many decades of planned effort to reduce the concentration of income. Thus, inequalities have been increasing in India during the last many decades neglecting the motto enshrined in the directive principles of our constitution. It was in this context that the government of India adopted economic reforms to boost the low economic growth of India. Those who are critical of reforms argue that economic reforms will increase the already existing high inequality in India. Hence, we have made an attempt to analyse the impact of reforms on inequality in India during the post reform period.

Although inequality is generally measured in terms of income, this inequality in income will be reflected in the standard of living of the people only when this is spent. Therefore, inequality in the consumption expenditure is a better indicator of the differences in the standard of living.

In our attempt to examine the inequality in India during the post reform period, we have examined inequality in terms of consumption. Table 3 depicts the consumption inequality in India during the post reform period. It can be seen from the table that the consumption share of first quintile in rural India has increased from 9.3 per cent in 1987-88 to 9.6 per cent in 1993-94 and to 10.1 per cent in 1999-2000 whereas the share of 5th quintile has declined from 39.6 per cent in 1987-88 to 38.5 per cent in 1993-94 and to 36.7 per cent in 1999-2000 (table 3).

Table 3
Trend in Consumption Inequality in India During the Post reform Period

Consumption Distribution, NSS	*1987-88*	*1993-94*	*1999-2000*
Rural			
Share of			
Quintile 1	9.3	9.6	10.1
Quintile 2	13.2	13.5	14.0
Quintile 3	16.5	16.9	17.3
Quintile 4	21.4	21.6	21.9
Quintile 5	39.6	38.5	36.7
Gini	29.9	28.6	26.3
Urban			
Share of			
Quintile 1	8.0	8.0	7.9
Quintile 2	11.7	11.9	11.7
Quintile 3	15.5	15.7	15.7
Quintile 4	21.4	21.6	21.7
Quintile 5	43.4	42.8	43.0
Gini	35.0	34.4	34.7
National			
Share of			
Quintile 1	8.6	8.7	8.9
Quintile 2	12.4	12.4	12.6
Quintile 3	15.8	15.9	16.0
Quintile 4	21.1	21.1	21.1
Quintile 5	42.1	41.8	41.4
Gini	32.9	32.5	32.0

Source: Surjith S Bhalla, EPW 2003.

The Gini has improved sharply in rural India as it fell from 29.9 in 1987-88 to 28.6 in 1993-94 and to 26.3 in 1999-2000. As such, inequality in rural areas during the post reform p period has declined considerably.

In urban India, the consumption share of first quintile is almost stagnant from 8 per cent in 1987-88 to 8 per cent in 1993-94 and to 7.9 per cent in 1999-2000 and the share of the fifth quintile also remained stagnant at 43.4 per cent in 1987-88 and to 42.8 per cent in 1993-94 and to 43 per cent in 1999-2000. The urban Gini has also slightly improved from 35 in 19987-88 to 34.4 in 1993-94 and then slightly increased to 34.7.

In India (rural plus urban), the consumption share of first quintile has increased from 8.6 per cent in 1987-88 to 8.7 per cent in 1993-94 and to 8.9 per cent in 1999-2000 whereas the share of fifth quintile has declined from 42.1 per cent in 1987-88 to 41.8 per cent in 1993-94 and to 41.4 per cent in 1999-2000. The Gini has slightly improved from 32.9 in 1987-88 to 32.5 in 1993-94 and to 32 in 1999-2000. Thus, it can be safely concluded that consumption inequality in India during the post reform period has declined and the trend is towards greater equality.

CONCLUSION

Economic reforms were initiated to accelerate the economic growth of the country. The new measures will have varied effects in the country especially on economic growth, inter-state disparities in growth and inequality. The paper analysed the impact of reforms on economic growth and inequality in the growth rates among states apart from analysing the inequality in consumption in India. We have examined the growth rate in terms of annual growth rates in Gross National Product (GNP FC), Net National Product (NNP FC), Per capita Net National Product (PNNP FC) and Real Gross Domestic Product (GDP FC). The post reform economic growth in India shows that economic reforms in India have accelerated economic growth.

Our examination of interstate disparities in economic growth shows wide disparities in the rates of growth among the states. The performance of 15 states are higher than the growth of all states GSDP while 12 states annual compound growth rates are lower than the growth rate of all states. The coefficient of variation for all states is 28.14 per cent whereas it is 27.94 per cent for 16 major states. Sixteen states could achieve a higher growth rate of NSDP higher than the growth rate for all states while 11 states growth rates are below the average growth rate of all states during the post reform period. The per capita NSDP growth rate of 14 states are more than the all states per capita NSDP growth rates while 13 states per capita NSDP growth rates are below the all states per capita NSDP growth rates. The coefficient of variation among states in GSDP is 28.14 per cent, per capita GSDP is 52.19 per cent, NSDP is 32.00 per cent and per capita NSDP is 56.39 per cent. So reforms have resulted in unequal growth rates and interstate disparities in growth rates.

Our analysis of inequality shows that inequality has declined in India during the post reform period and the trend is towards greater equality.

REFERENCES

Ahluwalia, Montek S. (2000), 'Economic Reforms: A Policy Agenda for the Future', in Economic Development in India, Vol. 25 (Academic Foundation).

Atkinson, A.B. (1983), "The Economics of Inequality" Clarendon Press, Oxford.

Bhalla, Surjith S. (2003), Recounting the Poor: Poverty in India, 1983-99' *Economic and Political Weekly*, January 25, 2003, pp. 338-349.

Economic Survey (2004-05), Government of India, P-S4.

Jha, Raghabendra, 'Growth, Inequality and Poverty in India Spatial and Temporal Characteristics' *Economic and Political Weekly*, March 11, 2000, pp. 921-928.

Panagariya, Arvind (2004), Growth and Reforms During 1980s and 1990's, *Economic and Political Weekly*, June 19,2004, pp. 2581-2594.

Rao Govinda, Shand R.T. and Kalirajan K.P. (1999), "Convergence of Incomes across Indian States A Divergent View", *Economic and Political Weekly*, March 27, 1999, pp. 769-778.

Shetty S.L. (2003), Growth of SDP and Structural Changes in State Economics Interstate Comparisons, *Economic and Political Weekly*, December 6, 2003, pp. 5189-5200.

Sundaram K. and Tendulkar Suresh D. (2003), Poverty in India in the 1990's An Analysis of Changes in 15 Major States, *Economic and Political Weekly*, April 5, 2003, pp. 1385-1393.

P. KRISHNA KUMAR AND C.A. PRIYESH

Economic Reforms and Regional Disparity

8

PART - I

REGIONAL DISPARITIES IN INDIA: A MACRO LEVEL PROFILE

Balanced regional growth is necessary for the harmonious development of a federal state such as India. Balanced regional development does not mean equal development of all regions in the country. It simply implies the fullest development of the potentialities of an area according to its capacity so that the inhabitants of all the regions can share the benefits of overall economic growth. India, however, presents a picture of extreme regional variations, in terms of the indicators of economic growth such as per capita income, the proportion of population living below the poverty line and other important socio-economic indicators. Relatively speaking, some states are economically advanced while others are relatively backward. The co-existence of relatively developed and backward states (interms of economic and social development) in a country is known as regional disparity. Regional disparity or regional imbalance may be natural due to unequal natural endowments. Some times it may be man-made in the sense of neglect of some regions and preference of others for investment and development effort. Regional disparity may be inter-state or intrastate; they may be total or sectoral. Economic backwardness of a region is indicated by symptoms like high pressure of population on land, excessive dependence on agriculture leading to high incidence of rural unemployment and underemployment, absence of large-scale urbanization, low productivity in agriculture and cottage industries

A THEORETICAL EXPLANATION OF REGIONAL DISPARITY

Underdeveloped countries are characterized by regional differences in income and employment. According to G. Myrdal (1958) the main cause of regional inequalities has been the strong backwash effects and the weak spread effects in such economies. The genesis of regional inequalities has a non-economic basis that is associated with the capitalist system guided by the profit motive. The profit motive results in the development of those regions where the prospects of profit are high while other regions remain underdeveloped.

Myrdal attributes the phenomenon to the free play of market forces. The latter tend to concentrate economic and social overheads in certain regions leaving the rest of the country in a backwater. Migration, capital movements and trade accentuate these inequalities. Migration of young and active people from the backward regions will favour the advanced region and depress economic activity in the former; capital will move into the developed regions thereby creating capital shortage in the backward region. So the backwash effects being stronger than the spread effects, regional inequalities are accentuated.

INDICATORS OF REGIONAL IMBALANCE

Regional imbalances in some Indian states are analyzed below. The selected states are Punjab, Gujarat, West Bengal, Karnataka, Kerala, Maharashtra, Haryana, Tamil Nadu, Andhra Pradesh, Madhya Pradesh, Assam, Uttar Pradesh, Rajasthan, Orissa and Bihar. Among these states, the first nine states are advanced states and the remaining are backward states. Punjab tops on the list as it has the highest per capita income and Bihar is at the bottom in the list of backward states as it has the lowest per capita income Net State Domestic Product, Per capita income, life expectancy, infant mortality rate, birth rate death rate and proportions of poor below poverty line are major indicators of regional disparity. Based on these indicators, the performances of 15 selected Indian states (nine developed and six poor states) are analyzed below to highlight the extent of regional disparity in India. In 1980-81, out of a total net domestic income of Rs.110340 crores for the whole country, the nine forward states accounted for 55%, while the six backward states accounted for nearly 39 per cent. But in 1997-98, the same forward states raised their share to 58 per cent, while the share of the 6 backward states in net national product declined to 27 per cent (Table 1). In other words, the richer states are becoming more advanced, while the backward states are becoming still poorer and backward.

Table 1
State wise Net State Domestic Product at Factor cost
(At 1980-81 Prices)

	Rs. Crore			Annual Average Growth Rate	
State	*1980-81*	*1990-91*	*1997-98*	*1980-81 to 1990-91*	*1990-91 to 1997-98*
Advanced States					
Punjab	4449	7505	10142	5.3	4.4
Maharashtra	15163	27244	42932	6.0	6.7
Haryana	3032	5719	7545	6.5	6.7
Gujarat	6547	10839	18433	5.2	7.9
West Bengal	9594	14458	22767	4.2	6.7
Karnataka	5587	9112	13683	5.0	6.0
Kerala	3823	5262	7782	3,2	5.8
TamilNadu	7218	12423	18193	5.6	5.6
AndhraPradesh	7324	11723	17936	4.8	6.3
Sub-total	62737 (55.0)	104265 (54.8)	159413 (57.8)	5.2	6.3
Backwardstates					
Madhya Pradesh	7012	11107	14748	4.7	4.1
Assam	2298	3426	4302	4.1	3.3
Uttar Pradesh	14012	22780	27365	5.0	2.6
Rajasthan	4126	8473	11138	7.4	4.0
Orissa	3443	4345	6013	2.3	4.7
Bihar	6349	10253	10653	4.9	3.0
Sub-Total	37240 (38.8)	60384 (31.7)	74219 (26.9)	4.9	3.0
All-India	110340 (100)	190218 (100)	275895 (100)	5.6	5.5

Source: Economic Survey (Various Issues).

The planning process, by helping the backward regions, made several attempts to reduce regional disparities, but the forces of liberalization and globalization strengthened investment in forward states and to a greater extent neglected the backward states. Consequently, regional disparities in growth rates widened further.

Per Capita Net State Domestic Products as the Indicator of Regional Disparity

Table 2 reveals per capita NSDP at 1993-94 prices for both forward and backward states. Punjab has highest per capita income both in 1990-91 and in 2000-01.Orissa had the lowest per capita income in 1990-91, but in 2000-01, Bihar recorded the lowest per capita income.

Table 2
Per Capita Net State Domestic Product at Factor Cost
(At 1980-81 Prices)

State	*1990-91 (Rs.)*	*2000-01 (Rs.)*	*Annual Average Growth Rate 1990-91 to 2000-01*
Forward StatesPunjab	11779	15390	2.7
Maharastra	10248	15172	4.0
Haryana	11125	14331	2.6
Gujarat	8788	12975	3.9
West Bengal	6013	9778	5.0
Karnataka	6629	11910	6.0
Kerala	6851	10712	4.6
Tamil Nadu	7872	12779	4.9
Andhra Pradesh	6873	9982	3.8
BACKWARDSTATES			
Madhya pradesh	6321	7003	1.0
Assam	5574	6157	1.0
Uttar Pradesh	5342	5770	0.8
Rajasthan	6771	7937	1.6
Orissa	4300	5187	1.9
Bihar	4476	3345	-2.8
All-India	7321	10254	3.4
Ratio between Maximum and Minimum Per capita NSDP	2.74	4.60	

Source: Economic Survey (Various Issues).

In seven out of the nine forward states under study, the annual average growth rate of per capita income between 1991 -2001 is higher than the all India average where as in all backward states it is much lower than the national average. The ratio of gap between maximum and minimum per capita income has increased much during the post-reform period. During the Pre-reform period it was 2.74 and it has almost doubled i.e., to 4.60 in the post-reform period indicating the increase in regional disparity.

Table 3
Selected Indicators of Human Development for Major States

States	*Life Expectancy at birth (2001-06)*		*Infant Mortality Rate (Per 1000 live birth) (2002)*			*Birth rate per 1000*	*Death rate per 1000*
	Male	*Female*	*Male*	*Female*	*Total*	*2000*	*2000*
Forward States			38	66	51	20.8	7.1
Punjab	69.78	72.00					
Maharastra	66.75	69.76	48	42	45	20.3	7.3
Haryana	64.64	69.30	54	73	62	26.6	7.1
Gujarat	63.12	64.10	55	66	60	24.7	7.7
West Bengal	66.08	69.34	53	45	49	20.5	6.7
Karnataka	62.43	66.44	56	53	55	22.1	7.2
Kerala	71.67	75.00	9	12	10	16.9	6.4
Tamil Nadu	67.00	69.75	46	43	44	18.5	7.7
Andhra Pradesh	62.79	65.00	64	60	62	20.7	8.5
Backwardstates							
Madhya Pradesh	59.19	58.01	81	88	85	30.4	9.8
Assam	58.96	60.87	70	71	70	26.6	9.2
Uttar Pradesh	63.54	64.09	76	84	80	31.6	9.7
Rajasthan	62.17	62.80	75	80	78	30.6	7.7
Orissa	60.05	59.71	95	79	87	23.2	9.8
Bihar	65.00	64.79	56	66	61	30.9	7.9
All-India	63.87	66.91	62	65	63	25.0	8.1

Source: India Development Report-2003 & 2004.

Selected Social Indicators

Selected indicators of human development also reinforce the regional disparity in the country. Infant mortality rate, birth rate and death rate are higher in the backward states than in the forward states. It clearly establishes the socio - economic inequality in India.

Percentage of population below poverty line in all the forward states except Tamil Nadu is always lower than the all India average whereas it is above the all India average in the backward states. Poor performance of human development indicators and high proportion of the people below poverty line indicates that the social as well as income status of the people in the backward states are very poor compared to the forward states. In other words it can be said that regional imbalance will result in social and income inequality that will distort the quality of life and well being of the people.

Table 4
Percentage of Population below Poverty Line of the major States over the Years

State	*1983-84*	*1987-88*	*1993-94*	*1999-2000*
Forward States Punjab	16.18	12.7	11.77	6.16
Maharastra	43.44	40.1	36.86	25.02
Haryana	21.37	16.63	25.05	8.74
Gujarat	32.79	32.33	24.21	14.07
West Bengal	54.85	43.99	35.66	27.02
Karnataka	38.24	38.14	33.16	20.04
Kerala	40.42	32.08	25.43	12.72
Tamil Nadu	54.79	51.66	45.13	35.03
Andhra Pradesh	28.91	27.20	22.19	15.77
Backwardstates				
Madhya pradesh	49.78	43.40	42.52	37.43
Uttar Pradesh	47.07	41.99	4.085	31.15
Rajasthan	34.46	34.60	27.41	15.28
Orissa	65.29	55.61	48.56	47.15
Bihar	62.22	53.37	54.96	42.60
All-India	44.80	39.34	36	26

Source: Economic Surveys (Relevant years).

Causes for Economic Backwardness and Regional Imbalances

There are certain deterrent factors that come in the way of rapid development of a region. Most important of these are the geographical isolation, inadequacy of economic overheads like transport, labour, technology and lack of access to basic amenities of life.

Historically, the existence of backward regions started from the British rule in India. The British helped the development of only those regions that possessed facilities for prosperous manufacturing and trading activities. Maharashtra and West Bengal were the states preferred by the British industrialists. The three metropolitan cities–Calcutta, Bombay and Madras–attracted all the industries and the rest of the country was neglected and remained backward. The uneven investment in irrigation during the British period helped some areas to become prosperous at the expense of the development of other areas.

New investment, more so, in the private sector has a tendency to concentrate in an already well-developed area, thus reaping the benefit of external economies. This is but natural from the private sector point of view, since well-developed areas offers private investors certain basic advantages such as infrastructural facilities, transport and market. In India regional disparities has been serious since Independence. Efforts are being taken by the government to reduce the regional disparities. For this special schemes were introduced in economic plans. To some extent the Finance Commissions also dealt with this issue. The growing regional disparity in the post-reform period is now a matter of serious concern. All the efforts made at the macro level to reduce the regional imbalances were been badly influenced by the New Economic Reforms of 1991 that strengthened the market forces. With deregulation of private investment, faster growth will induce investment, and this in turn will further accentuate disparity. The problem is compounded by the negative relationship between population growth and income during the 1990s (Bhattacharya & Sakthivel, 2004).

This regional disparity leads to the prevalence of high poverty, unemployment, unplanned migration, food insecurity and social problems like naxalism and some movements that stand even for the disintegration of our country. But this study limits its scope to inter-state disparity in the distribution of food grains through the public distribution system (PDS) and the impact of globalization and related economic reforms that we introduced since 1991 on the performance PDS across the states.

PART - II

THE CASE FOR PUBLIC DISTRIBUTION SYSTEM IN INDIA

Food is the basic need of human life. Since food is an economic good the price mechanism operates in its case also. Supply constraints and high demand pushes up the price of food items. As the economic theory tells, in a free market economy, a few/ large proportion of consumers demand and supply is influenced by a few/large proportion of producers and the equilibrium price is always determined by the interaction of supply and demand. But the problem among consumers arises when a certain group of them are not able to pay this equilibrium price. Lack of entitlement leads to inadequate food consumption, malnutrition and even starvation. Even in a dual price market for food grains this problem persists when the prices set by the government is higher and unaffordable to certain groups of consumers. So food insecurity is a pertinent issue for human beings in general and vulnerable sections of the society in particular.

A paradoxical phenomenon observed in India is that even when there is enough food to prevent death due to starvation, individuals may not be able to consume sufficient food to enable them to lead a full life or achieve their maximum productivity. (Sen 1999; Chowdhary, 1998). According to NSSO (1999-2000) studies, even though sufficient food grains are produced in India, 26 per cent of the population lives below the poverty line. In this context the need for PDS assumes paramount significance. PDS in India was initiated as an ad-hoc wartime measure to make food grains accessible to the people at affordable prices. Now it has turned out as the largest system that ensures food security.

The low-income rural households mainly depend on the local markets for purchasing food items and the time element is a crucial variable that influences their demand. During and a few month following the harvest, food grains are available at affordable prices and in general then rural households are self sufficient in food. But during the remaining months of the year the pressure in the market increases as most of the households exhaust their own stocks and begin to depend heavily on the market. Fluctuations in the price of food grains and its non-availability are aggravated by the speculative bahaviour of the traders. In order to meet their food expense in the lean season poor households are forced to take loans at exorbitant rates of interest from local moneylenders. PDS plays a pivotal role in safeguarding the interests of the poor households by making food grain available at reasonable prices to the consumers through public distribution out lets.

Under-nutrition and Chronic Energy Deficiency (CED) are serious health hazards in many Indian states. The regional disparities highlighted in the states in the first part of this study are reflected in Calorie deficiency, CED and Under-nutrition also. National Nutrition Monitory Bureau (NNMB-2001) data shows that 37.4 per cent of adult males and 39.4 per cent of adult females in 2000-2001 suffered CED in many Indian States.

(See Appendix Table 9, 10, 11, and 12) In terms of the nutritional status of children, middle–income states such as Kerala, Tamil Nadu, and Andhra Pradesh performed better than higher–income states like Maharastra, Gujarat and West Bengal. Not surprisingly, poorer states such as Madhya Pradesh and Orissa showed the worst performance.

The interstate variations in CED are similar to those of malnutrition among children. CED was found to be lower in Kerala (22.4 per cent for males and 18.7 per cent for females) and in Tamil Nadu (26.7 per cent for males and 38.7 per cent for females) and higher in Madhya Pradesh, Maharastra, and West Bengal (above 50 per cent). (See Appendix Table 9, 10, 11 and 12).

Gender differences seem to exist in some states, particularly Tamil Nadu. NFHS–2 shows that 36 per cent of ever-married women aged 15–49 years have chronic energy deficiency It is more pronounced among rural women, illiterate women and women surviving in a low standard of living situation (India Development Report, 2004). CED levels are higher in Maharashtra, Gujarat and West Bengal and are closer to that of less developed states like Bihar, Madhya Pradesh and Orissa. Punjab, Kerala, Arunachal Pradesh, Manipur and Nagaland have lower incidence of female malnutrition. The study of National Council for Applied Economic Research (NCAER, 1999) on under nutrition shows that about 37 per cent of children aged 0–4 years suffer from stunting. Stunting is higher in Karnataka, Madhya Pradesh, Gujarat, Andhra Pradesh, Haryana and West Bengal in comparison with Kerala and Tamil Nadu. Death due to starvation is increasing in the country. Consumption of cereals, the major source of energy has on an average declined (Chand, 2005). Consumption expenditure of 26 per cent of Indians is BPL.Expenditure on food is the largest component in the family budget in majority of the Indian households. Expenditure on food is more than 60 per cent of family budget in the urban area and it is 80 per cent in the rural area. (Kabra & Ittyerah, 1992).

Evidence on the consumption of food, on calorie intake, and on nutritional outcomes clearly establishes that chronic hunger persists on a mass scale in India. The persistence of hunger and malnutrition, on such a large scale is the principal justification for strengthening a system of food distribution through PDS .In a country where there is mass poverty, where food consumption is low, where about half the adults and children suffer malnutrition and where expenditure on food accounts for the bulk of total family expenditure, we need to expand and strengthen–and not to undermine or dilute–effective policies of food security.

Theoretical Justification for PDS

In a private sector dominated economy both personal and functional distribution of income are subject to a certain degree of inequality due to various distortions in the factor market and commodity market. Theoretical conditions for achieving perfect equality do not exist in such an economy. Complete information on the part of economic agents, perfect flexibility of factor prices and commodity prices are some of these important conditions. On the side of consumption the private sector dominated economy does not help to satisfy the condition of optimality–the equality of marginal rate substitution of commodities among all consumers. Distribution is efficient only when this Pareto condition is satisfied. PDS can be defined as a system that with help of private distribution system attempts to achieve the above Pareto condition of efficient distribution.

Due to basic inequality in the distribution of income and purchasing power among economic agents the marginal rate of substitution of commodities for all people are not equal. Without correcting the inequality in the distribution of income and purchasing power the PDS makes a direct attempt in subsidizing the commodities so that those who are on the lower levels of the income scale are enabled to equate their marginal rate of substitution of commodities with the price they pay and also equate the marginal rate of substitution of commodities among themselves.

Demand—Supply Framework of PDS in Food Grains Management

The public distribution of food grains, which is a significant component of food security system in the country, is expected to influence the market prices and reduce the fluctuations therein, by regulating the supply in line with the demand. In the peak marketing period, the availability (supply) of food grains increases, resulting into depression in market prices. However, with a view to protecting the interest of the farmers, the prices are not allowed to fall to unremunerative levels by undertaking purchase operations by the public agencies at pre-determined support prices. From the consumers' viewpoint, the availability of the food grains is critically important during the lean marketing period. Therefore, the food grains are distributed on a larger scale during lean period to reduce the pressure on prices in the open market. The impact of the public intervention on food grain marketing, both in peak and lean marketing period is shown in Figure 1.

Figure 1
Peak Season Intervention

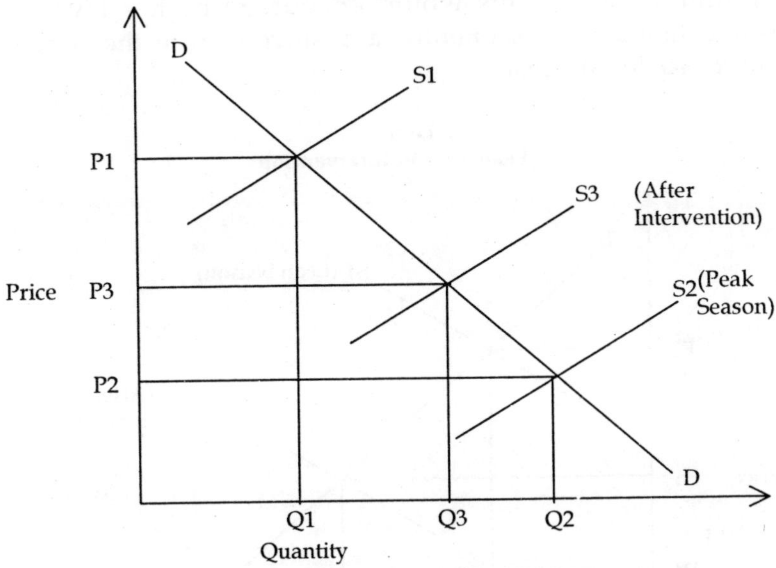

The changing price situation during the peak marketing season as a result of the state intervention in food grains marketing is shown in Figure 1 The normal equilibrium price is determined at the intersection of the demand (DD) and supply (S1) curves at price P1 and quantity Q1. During the peak marketing season, as a result of increased availability, the supply curve (S1) shifts downward to the right to S2 and the new equilibrium price is established at price P2 and quantity Q2.Thus, during the peak season, there is a fall in price from P1 to P2. With a view to avoiding the situation of sharp decline in price, the public agencies intervene through undertaking procurement/price support operations, at a pre-decided price P3, a quantity (Q2–Q3) is procured by the public agencies. This, in turn, reduces the availability in the open market and consequently the supply curve S2 shifts towards the left to S3. As a result, the new market equilibrium is established at price P3, there by ensuring that the price of food grains in the post harvest period do not decline to unremunerative prices to the farmers.

Apart from helping in the allocation of the resources in an optimum manner,this would encourage higher level of production and consequently, a positive shift in the supply curve would take place.

Figure 2
Lean Season Intervention

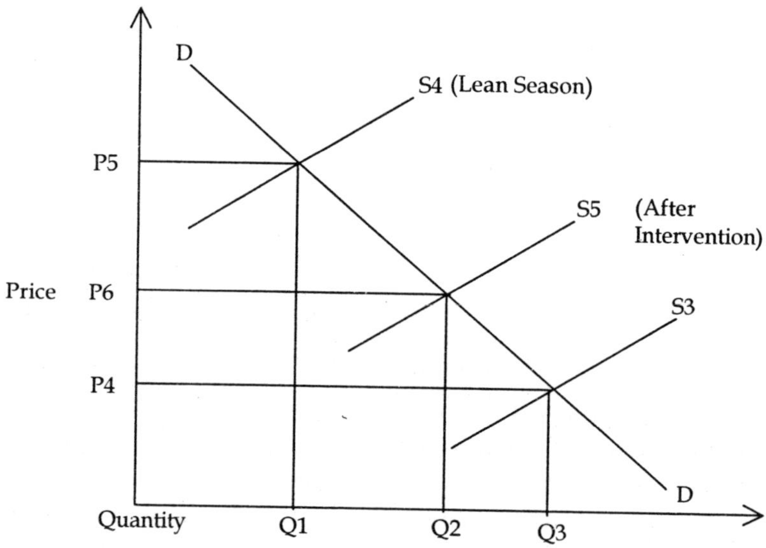

During the lean season, due to the reduced availability, the supply curve shifts towards the left from S3 to S4 and the new equilibrium price is established at price P5 at quantity Q1 as shcwn in Figure 2. This high price adversely affects the consumers as their purchasing power gets eroded.. In order to mitigate their suffering, state intervention through PDS is activated on a large scale resulting in improved availability. The supply curve S4 shifts to S3 as a result of releases from the buffer stocks to the extent of (Q1–Q2), thus bringing down the price from P5 to P6.Thus, the state intervention through procurement and public distribution of food grains safeguards the interest not only of the farmers but also of the consumers in general. The magnitude of the difference in the two prices i.e., P5 and P6 will depend on the scale of intervention and the difference between the PDS price and the open market price. Also a larger proportion of the total quantity of food grains distributed to the poor and to the deficit areas will help in bringing down the prices to a more reasonable level.

Economic Reforms and Public Distribution System

The shift in the policy objectives of the Government of India after the introduction of Structural Adjustment Programmes in 1991 has created major threat to the smooth functioning of PDS in the country and this has been reflected in the state. Reformers considered most subsidies including food subsidy as a waste, and several changes in food policy were introduced. Economic Survey 1992-93 of the Government of India stated that while PDS has to be continued to help the poor, the subsidy on the central budget has to be restrained. Later, reformers have realized that a cut in food subsidy will lead to increased deprivation. Therefore, food subsidy was raised from Rs. 2800 crores in 1992-93 to Rs. 8200 crores in 1999-2000 and to Rs. 26500 in 2004-05. In a study, Madhura Swaminathan (2000) pointed out that these reforms have resulted in a steady increase in food price and a decline in the supply of food to the distribution system.

The procurement price of food grains in the country is influenced by political considerations. A strong agricultural lobby in the northern states such as Uttar Pradesh, Punjab and Haryana play a crucial role in this field. On several occasions, procurements have been made without considering the actual needs and the existing buffer stock. This system has adversely affected the efficiency of the PDS and has contributed to the rise in PDS prices.The introduction of revamped PDS has also created problems. Revamped PDS aims at targeting specific areas with special preferences given to people living in difficult areas. During the period of non-revamped PDS, entitlement was fixed on an individual basis, but under revamped PDS, a uniform ceiling per household per month (20 kilograms) was fixed. This strategy actually reduced the entitlement of households with a large number of members. With lower entitlements and higher prices, it is not surprising that the quantity of commodities sold through fair price shops have fallen since 1991.

Targeted PDS (TPDS) is different from the earlier programmes. Under this programme, a distinction between below-poverty-line (BPL) and above-poverty-line (APL) population is made. These two groups are treated differently with respect to the quantity allotted as well as the price charged. The Government of India has targeted PDS for BPL category, and entitlement has been altered from per capita norm to family norm.

Identifying and targeting the poor on the basis of the 'income criterion' has several limitations. Furthermore, since the official poverty line in India is fixed at a very low level, a household that receives ten or fifteen rupees more than that of the identified poor for TPDS cannot be considered as better off than them. By hiding the actual income figures, some people can also be got included in the BPL category. Mis-identification of households may lead to mis-targeting. After the introduction of TPDS, the price of rice distributed through fair price shops shot up and, in Kerala–the best performing state in PDS, it is now either very close to or even a little higher than the open-market price. So now the APL category consumers prefer to make purchases from the open market than from PDS. The quantity of rice sold through PDS is much inferior to that available in the open market. The fall in demand for PDS rice has created a glut and has resulted in loss forth.

PERFORMANCE OF PUBLIC DISTRIBUTION SYSTEM IN THE PRE AND POST REFORM PERIOD

State Wise Analysis

This part looks into the performance of PDS in the pre and post reform period in the major states of India. Here, performance means the participation (off take) of states in the distribution of food grains. The period of analysis is 21years, i.e. from 1980–2001. The whole period is divided into two on the basis of major changes in the economic policy and policy related to the working of public distribution system. Even though reforms on PDS were introduced in 1992 and vital changes happened in 1997, the government of India fully accepted the philosophy behind major changes on PDS management in 1991 itself. So the whole period of 21 years from 1980 to 2001 is divided into two: Pre–reform period of 1980 to 1991 and post–reform period of 1991 to 2001. This part seriously looks into how the off take of states behaves after the introduction of reforms on PDS in 1992 and 1997 as part of the Structural Adjustment Programmes and Stabilization Policies (Economic Reforms) of 1991.

The four southern-states, Andhra Pradesh, Tamil Nadu, Kerala and Karnataka (advanced states) stand out in terms of the distribution of food grain; accounting for almost one-half (48.7 per cent) of total PDS off takes of food grain in the country. The four northern states, Bihar, Madhya Pradesh, Rajasthan and Uttar Pradesh (or BIMARU states) accounted together for only 10 per cent of total national off take. These inter-state differences in the scale of PDS operations have persisted over many years (Madhura Swaminathan, 2000). Performance of PDS in the pre-reform and post-reform periods is analyzed below. The analysis brings out the non-uniformity in the coverage of PDS in different states during the period.

The off take of food grains by the advanced states in the pre-reform period has substantially increased. The two states, Punjab and Haryana are food surplus states, so they need not take huge quantity of food grains from the central pool. But by the end of 1980s there were general declines in food grains off take from the central pool. The increased off take by the richer states in the middle of 1980s shows the expansion of PDS in those states (table 5).

The performance of PDS in the advanced states in the Post-reform period shows some interesting trend. The 'Model state for PDS' in India–Kerala, has been performed very badly in the post-reform period (table 6). The nationally and even internationally acclaimed PDS in Kerala has been ruined by the economic reforms. The off take of food grains by West Bengal also declined substantially. But Tamil Nadu, Andhra Pradesh and Karnataka could perform well in the post-reform period.

Table 5
Food Grain off take of the Advanced States in the Pre-reform period (Qty 000 tonnes)

State Year	*Kerala*	*T.N.*	*A.P.*	*Gujarat*	*West Bengal*	*Maha-rashtra*	*Karna-taka*	*Punjab*	*Har-yana*
1980-81	925	659	548	354	2329	1561	574	324	140
81-82	1185	1168	589	426	2112	1605	671	209	95
82-83	1272	1246	628	460	2820	1581	701	330	188
83-84	1545	1580	1287	362	2944	1545	655	291	209
84-85	1536	1611	1219	294	2142	1135	754	175	119
85-86	1596	2147	1398	494	1925	1340	973	217	177
86-87	1824	1727	1707	837	2205	1773	1166	142	140
87-88	1821	1685	1525	1239	1717	1828	1023	317	126
88-89	1839	993	1005	1244	1871	1832	863	24	179
89-90	1486	926	1031	733	1479	1863	750	10	86
90-91	1560	913	1319	831	1526	1616	854	9	30

Source: Bulletin on food statistics (various years), Directorate of Economics and Statistics, Ministry of Agriculture, Government of India.

Table 6
Food Grains off take of the Advanced States in the Post-reform period (Qty 000 tonnes)

State Year	*Kerala*	*T.N.*	*A.P.*	*Gujarat*	*West Bengal*	*Maha-rashtra*	*Karna-taka*	*Punjab*	*Har-yana*
1991-92	2058	1168	1746	134	1525	1953	1034	93	174
92-93	2090	937	2407	997	1329	1946	1059	77	182
93-94	2036	962	2289	560	1189	1186	917	16	91
94-95	1484	1416	2432	629	1177	919	943	12	60
95-96	1654	1722	2378	654	1305	936	1207	870	68
96-97	2080	1484	2152	1397	1517	1657	1568	1018	168
97-98	2126.2	1519.3	2123.4	652.7	1268.4	1713	1197.3	39	102.8
98-99	2174	1617	2266	704	344	1939	1328	58	131
99-00	1727	2072	2602	749	381	2305	1343	30	314
2000-01	905	1771	2794	918	389	1562	1436	30	219

Source: Bulletin on food statistics (various years), Directorate of Economics and Statistics, Ministry of Agriculture, Government of India.

All backward states in the pre-reform period show very poor off take compared to the advanced states. It is observed that the poverty ratio is very high in these poor states Poverty ratios of all these poor states were higher than the national average (table 4). The socio-economic problems like malnutrition, CED, high IMR, high birth rate and high death rate may be the indirect results of the poor performance of PDS. (Appendix tables 1, 2, 3 & 4).

Table 7
Food Grain off take of the Backward States in the Pre-reform period (Qty 000 tonnes)

Year State	*Uttar Pradesh*	*Madhya Pradesh*	*Rajasthan*	*Orissa*	*Bihar*
1980-81	1893	1102	520	594	1006
81-82	542	542	194	291	555
82-83	1000	472	213	414	734
83-84	956	457	109	452	932
84-85	508	255	42	272	600
85-86	975	398	292	399	633
86-87	822	593	884	296	777
87-88	954	830	1263	416	1020
88-89	1156	598	1129	543	844
89-90	718	557	655	440	690
90-91	963	519	603	446	455

Source: Bulletin on food statistics (various years), Directorate of Economics and Statistics, Ministry of Agriculture, Government of India.

Table 8
Food Grain off take of the Backward States in the Post-reform period (Qty tonnes)

State	*Uttar Pradesh*	*Madhya Pradesh*	*Rajasthan*	*Orissa*	*Bihar*
1991-92	1028	616	883	554	701
92-93	1012	834	965	505	673
93-94	583	519	460	464	378
94-95	434	440	493	526	217
95-96	491	492	539	559	267
96-97	1974	1124	821	1124	772
97-98	1430.7	623.8	486.4	991	923.4
98-99	1715	782	589	1086	1030
99-00	1722	755	459	1009	903
2000-01	592	806	846	1303	903

Source: Bulletin on food statistics (various years), Directorate of Economics and Statistics, Ministry of Agriculture, Government of India.

Based on the available data, we cannot say that economic reform has deteriorated the performance of PDS in the poor

Chart 3
Organisational Structure of PDS in India

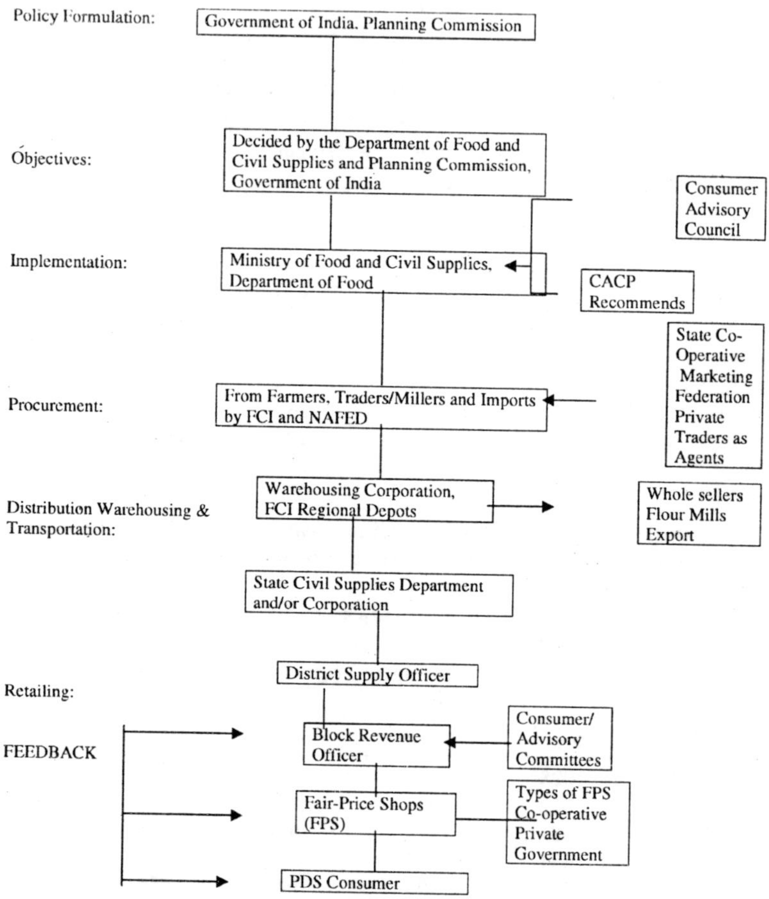

Source: Bapna (1990).

states. But it is very clear that, the reforms introduced on PDS such as RPDS and TPDS totally failed to ensure adequate and sufficient food grains to poor people in the backward states. In simple, the reforms increased the regional disparity in terms of Net State Domestic Product (NSDP) and Per capita Net State Domestic Product (PNSDP) and it could do nothing to safeguard the interest of BPL population in general and in the poor states in particular by providing sufficient food grains at affordable prices in time.

CONCLUSIONS

It is very clear that regional disparity is prevailing in India. Our five-year plans, the devolution of Finance Commissions and other financial assistance could not correct this disparity. Along with this, the economic reforms introduced since 1990 widened the disparity. The social indicators of backward states show the poor performance of them in terms of poverty eradication and addressing human development issues. One of the most important government policy measures to solve poverty, CED, malnutrition, etc., of all poor people across Indian states is PDS. The second part of this study seriously looked into the performance of PDS in the poor and rich states. Since regional disparity is widening and the absolute number of people below poverty line is increasing, a serious re-thinking is needed to improve the performance of PDS in India particularly in the backward states.

REFERENCES

Ahluwalia, Montek S. (2000), *Economic performance of States in Post-reforms period, Economic and Political Weekly,* March 6, pp. 1637-48.

Annual Report (2003–2004), Department of Food and Public Distribution, Ministry of Consumer Affairs, Food and Public Distribution, Government of India, New Delhi.

Bapna, S.L. (1990), *'Food Security Through the PDS: The Indian Experience'* in D.S. Tyagi and V.S. Vyas (eds.) Increasing Acess to Food: The Asian Experience, Sage Publications, New Delhi.

Bhattacharya, B.B. and S. Sakthivel (2004), *Regional Growth and disparity in India: Comparison of Pre-and Post-Reform Decades, Economic and Political Weekly,* March 6, pp. 1071-1077.

Bulletin on Food Statistics (various years), Directorate of Economics and Statistics, Ministry of Agriculture, Government of India.

Chand,Ramesh (2005), Whither India's Food Policy? From Food Security to Food Deprivation, *Economic and Political Weekly,* March 12.

Choudhry,R.C. and Raja Kutty (1998), Fifty Years of Rural Development in India: Retrospect and Prospect, (edited), National Institute of Rural Development, Hyderabad.

Dantawala, M.L. (1995), The Food Problem and the Green Revolution in Indian Economy, S. Chand & Company Ltd., New Delhi.

Dreze, Jean (2001), *"Right to Food and Public Accountability"*, The Hindu, December 5, pp. 8.

Economic Reviews and Economic Appraisals of Different States (Various years).

Economic Surveys (Various years), Ministry of Finance, Government of India.

George, P.S (1996)" *PDS, Food Subsidy and Production Incentives"*, *Economic and Political Weekly*, Set 28.

India Development Report, 2003-2004.

Kabra, Kamal Narayan and Anil Chandy Ittyerah (1992), *The Public Distribution System in India,* Eastern Books, New Delhi.

Krishna Kumar, P. (2002), Quality of Life at Households level of low Income Groups in Kerala, Unpublished Ph.D Thesis Submitted to the University of Kerala, Thiruvananthapuram.

Myrdal, G. (1958), *Economic Theory and Underdeveloped Regions.*

Parikh, Kirit S. (1994), *"Who Gets how much from PDS? How effectively does it reach the poor?"*. Sarvekshna, 58th Issue, January-March 1994.

Parikh, Kirit S. (ed.) (1997), *India Development Report*, Oxford University Press, New Delhi.

Rao, C.H. Hanumantha (2000), *"Declining Demand for foodgrain in Rural India: Causes and Implications"*, *Economic and Political Weekly*, January 22.

Sen,Amartya and Jean Dreze (1999), The Amartya Sen and Jean Dreze Omnibus-Essays on Poverty and Famines-Hunger and Public Action-India: Economic Development and Social Oppurnity, Oxford University Press,New Delhi.

Suryanarayana,M.H. (1991), Revamping of PDS Financial Express, August 22, 1991.

Swaminathan, Madura (2000), *"Weakening Welfare-The Public Distribution of Food in India"*, Left Word Books, New Delhi.

Tyagi, D.S. (1990), *"Managing India's Food Economy. Problems and Alternatives,"* sage Publications, New Delhi.

APPENDIX

Table 9
NFHS Estimates of Malnutrition among Children (Weight-for-age) and CED among Ever-married Women

State	*1993 (Children under four years)*			*1998-99 children under three years all (Rural + Urban)*	*CED among ever married women (age 15–49 years) (Rural+Urban)*
	Rural	*Urban*	*All*		
Andhra Pradesh	52.1	40.2	49.1	37.7	37.8
Bihar	64.1	53.8	62.6	54.4	39.7
Gujarat	45.8	40.5	44.1	45.1	37.6
Haryana	39.4	33.0	37.9	34.6	26.1
Himachal Pradesh	48.3	30.2	47.0	43.6	29.9
Jammu and Kashmir	NA	NA	44.5	34.5	26.6
Karnataka	NA	NA	NA	43.9	39.4
Kerala	30.6	22.9	28.5	26.9	18.9
Madhaya Pradesh	59.4	50.1	57.4	55.1	38.6
Maharashtra	57.5	45.5	52.6	49.6	40.3
Orissa	NA	NA	55.3	54.4	48.4
Punjab	47.4	40.0	45.9	28.7	17.0
Rajasthan	41.1	43.9	41.6	50.6	36.6
Tamil Nadu	52.1	32.3	46.6	36.7	29.3
UP	NA	NA	49.8	51.7	36.2
West Bengal	NA	NA	56.8	48.7	44.4
Arunachal Pradesh	40.3	36.2	39.7	24.3	11.1
Assam	51.8	37.3	50.4	36.0	27.1
Manipur	31.6	25.9	30.1	27.5	19.3
Meghalaya	47.2	37.5	45.5	37.9	25.7
Mizoram	34.5	22.0	28.1	27.7	22.8
Nagaland	30.5	19.7	28.7	24.1	18.7
Tripura	53.0	31.6	48.8	NA	35.7
All-India	59.9	45.2	53.4	47.0	36.2

Source: India Development Report – 2003.

Table 10
Incidence of Poverty–Statewise, 1993-94 and 1999-2000 (Rural & Urban)

(Percentages)

States	*1993 – 94*		*1999 – 2000*	
	Rural	*Urban*	*Rural*	*Urban*
All-India	36.8	32.8	26.5	24.0
Andhra Pradesh	15.9	38.8	10.5	27.2
Arunachal Pradesh	41.4	05.8	23.4	05.0
Assam	45.3	08.0	40.2	07.2
Bihar	57.9	34.8	44.0	33.5
Goa	05.0	28.2	00.0	06.3
Gujarat	22.1	28.3	12.4	14.8
Haryana	28.3	16.4	07.4	10.0
Himachal Pradesh	30.3	09.3	07.5	04.6
Jammu and Kashmir	18.2	05.1	04.7	02.0
Karnataka	30.2	39.8	16.9	24.6
Kerala	25.4	24.3	09.4	19.9
Madhya Pradesh	40.7	48.1	37.2	38.6
Maharashtra	37.9	35.0	23.3	26.8
Orissa	49.8	40.6	47.8	43.5
Punjab	11.7	10.8	06.0	05.4
Rajasthan	26.4	31.0	13.4	19.4
Tamil Nadu	33.0	39.9	20.1	22.5
UP	42.4	35.1	31.0	30.7
West Bengal	41.2	23.0	31.7	14.7
Delhi	02.0	16.1	0.70	09.2
Pondicherry	18.9	36.4	11.5	22.4

Source: India Development Report, 2003-2004.

Table 11
Under-nutrition (Height-for-age) among Poor and Incidence of Chronic Poverty: 1997-98

State category	*Rural*		*Urban*	
	Percentage of stunted children among poor	*Percentage of chronically poor*	*Percentage of stunted children among poor*	*Percentage of chronically poor*
Andhra Pradesh	49.6	05.2	34.3	13.5
Assam	52.4	21.1	49.1	03.8
Bihar	57.5	25.3	63.0	19.3
Gujarat	49.5	06.1	51.2	07.3

State category	*Rural*		*Urban*	
	Percentage of stunted children among poor	*Percentage of chronically poor*	*Percentage of stunted children among poor*	*Percentage of chronically poor*
Haryana	60.5	04.5	64.2	06.1
Himachal Pradesh	58.8	04.4	54.8	02.7
Jammu and Kashmir	59.9	02.8	51.6	01.2
Karnataka	56.5	09.6	49.7	13.9
Kerala	32.4	03.1	30.9	06.5
Madhya Pradesh	57.4	21.4	56.9	22.2
Maharashtra	55.8	13.0	30.9	15.0
Orissa	51.1	24.4	49.1	22.2
Punjab	56.9	03.4	46.4	03.1
Rajasthan	60.1	08.1	57.2	11.7
Tamil Nadu	41.6	08.4	46.5	09.4
West Bengal	60.0	19.0	53.5	08.8
U.P	63.1	19.6	59.6	19.4
Other States	43.1	05.3	46.4	03.9
All-India	57.1	15.1	49.6	13.7

Source: India Development Report, 2003.

Table 12
Under-nutrition among Children (aged 1-5 years) and CED among Adults in Rural Areas of Selected

State	*Period*	*Under nutrition (%)*	*CED*	
			Males	*Females*
Kerala	1975-79	56.8	22.4	18.7
	1991-92	35.6		
	2000-01	28.8		
Tamil Nadu	1975-79	59.6	26.7	38.2
	1991-92	47.4		
	2000-01	39.0		
Karnataka	1975-79	64.3	36.2	41.7
	1991-92	62.8		
	2000-01	47.7		
Andhra Pradesh	1975-79	61.5	37.4	42.0
	1991-92	50.8		
	2000-01	39.9		

Contd....

State	*Period*	*Under nutrition (%)*	*CED*	
			Males	*Females*
Maharashtra	1975-79	71.4	41.3	45.1
	1991-92	62.2		
	2000-01	55.2		
Gujarat	1975-79	68.1	37.1	33.3
	1991-92	62.3		
	2000-01	48.9		
Madhya Pradesh	1975-79	61.3	42.8	41.9
	2000-01	63.9		
Orissa	1975-79	56.6	38.6	46.0
	1991-92	58.8		
	2000-01	54.4		
West Bengal	1975-79	60.6	40.5	45.9
	2000-01	49.6		
All-States	1975-79	62.5	37.4	39.4
	1991-92	56.2		
	2000-01	50.5		

Source: India Development Report–2003.

Table 13
Procurement of Rice During 2003-2004

Year 2004

State	*Quantity Procured (in lakh tonnes)*	*% of Quantity Procured to Total Procurement*
Andhra Pradesh	23.76	12.56
Haryana	13.24	7.00
Madhya Pradesh	1.06	0.56
Orissa	7.23	3.82
Punjab	86.29	45.03
Rajasthan	0.39	0.21
Uttar Pradesh	21.81	11.53
Others	35.33	18.69

Source: Annual Report 2004–2005. Ministry of consumer Affairs, Food and Public Distribution System, Government of India.

Table 14
Procurement of Wheat During 2003-2004

Year 2004

State	*Quantity procured (in lakh tonnes)*	*% of Quantity procured to total procurement*
Haryana	51.22	32.41
Madhya Pradesh	1.88	1.19
Punjab	89.38	56.57
Rajasthan	2.59	1.64
Uttar Pradesh	12.13	7.68
Others	0.81	0.51

Source: Annual Report 2004–2005. Ministry of consumer Affairs, Food and Public Distribution System, Government of India.

V.K. VIJAYAKUMAR

Reforms, Growth and Poverty

9

INTRODUCTION

Poverty is the most heart rending of all economic problems. Being deprived of much of the basic necessities of life and well being is indeed, a very unfortunate state of affairs. Which is why, economists who seldom agree on economic issues, agree that poverty all over the world has to be eradicated at the earliest. Even though there is a consensus on the need to eradicate poverty, there is no consensus on how to do it.

What is poverty?

Traditionally, poverty has been defined in terms of material deprivation, that is, deprivation of the basic needs of food, clothing, housing etc. This deprivation caused by low consumption of these material needs, which in turn, is caused by low income, is only one dimension of the problem. There are other dimensions, equally pressing, to this problem. These include deprivation of education and health. Exposure and vulnerability to risk, viocelessness, powerlessness and marginalization are the other dimensions of poverty.

So..............
Being hungry is poverty
Not having shelter is poverty
Not having clothing is poverty
Being sick and not treated is poverty
Being illiterate and not schooled is poverty
Voicelessness is poverty

Powerlessness is poverty
Marginalization is poverty

All these are forms of poverty, because, they restrict the 'capabilities' of people the evolution of poverty.

Poverty is as old as mankind. Mankind has been living on earth for the last 2 million years. For 99.5% of these enos of human existence, man lived the life of hunter and gatherer. Then, just 10000years ago, agriculture was discovered and settled life began, leading to the drawn of civilization. With agricultural production, living conditions started improving, albeit very slowly.

It was industrial revolution, the so called 'Second wave' that led to tremendous increase in production, Productivity and prosperity. But in the initial years following the Industrial Revolution, inspite of the increasing production, there was no marked decline in poverty. For the vast majority of mankind, existence was at the substance level; life was a dreary toil from one day to the next. As late as 1820, about 75% of world population lived in poverty. This period was also characterized by low level of inequalities in the distribution of income and wealth. Around 1820, the lowest level of income and wealth was in China at $ 500 and the highest in Western Europe at $500 (calculated at current prices). Colonialism and imperialist exploitation added to the woes of poor people in many parts of the world.

From early 19th century to the present day, for a period encompassing around 200 years, poverty declined drastically. Of course, this decline in poverty was very uneven. Western Europe, the USA, Scandinavia, Japan and East Asia witnessed drastic reduction and even elimination of poverty while sub Saharan Africa experienced aggravation of poverty and South Asia, excluding China saw marginal decline in poverty. The period from 1980 to 2001 witnessed great reduction in poverty in certain regions and a small decline in others. See table 1.

It can be seen that between 1981 and 2001, the share of the population in developing and transitional economies living on less than $1 a day (the international measure of extreme poverty), fell from 40.4% to 20.7%. But one can see big regional variations in poverty. While poverty ratio declined in East Asia from 56.6 in 1981 to 14.3% in 2001, it increased in sub Saharan Africa during this period. Again while there is a sizeable decline in poverty ratio in the Middle East, North Africa and South Asia, there is stagnation in Latin America and the Caribbean. The increase in poverty in Europe and Central Asia happened in the case of countries in transition to market economies.

Table 1
Share of Population Living on less than $1 a day
(per cent)

Region	*1981*	*2001*
East Asia and Pacific	56.7	14.3
Europe and Central Asia	0.8	3.5
Latin America and the Caribbean	10.1	9.9
Middle East and North Africa	5.1	2.4
South Asia	51.5	31.9
Sub-Saharan Africa	41.6	46.4
Total	40.4	20.7

Source: World Bank 2000s.

Presently, the distribution of poor people (living on less $1 a day) is very uneven. While Western Europe, America and Scandinavian countries are devoid of poverty, there is heavy concentration of poverty in South Asia, Sub-Saharan Africa, East Asia and pacific.

GROWTH AND REFORMS

This brings us to the crucial question: what leads to growth? We have experience of the developed world and the presently developing world to learn from. Study of the policies and circumstances that led to growth in these economies reveals the fact that there is no single model that can lead to growth. The experience of North America, Western Europe, Japan, Scandinavia, the Asian tigers, China etc. reveal different models and policies. The role of the state and the markets were different in these economies. In USA and Western Europe, liberal politics and market economies lead to growth. In Japan and East Asia, the state did play a role, but the engine of growth has been private initiative and enterprise. It is important to note that in china growth really took off after the introduction of reforms in 1978. There fore, even though the models were different, one can discern some common characteristics running through these policies, viz., global integration, export promotion, market orient reforms, deregulation and decontrol, stable monetary and fiscal policies and full fledged encouragement of private initiative and enterprise. There fore, these policies can certainly be regarded as essential ingredients of a successful growth strategy. It is important to note that not a single centrally planned command economy based on comprehensive planning and public ownership of business enterprises succeeded in achieving high rates of growth.

REFORMS, GROWTH AND POVERTY: THE INDIAN EXPERIENCE

Data relating to growth and poverty in India is shown in Table 2.

Table 2
Incidence of Poverty in India

Year	*Poverty ratio (%)*	*No. of poor (in million)*
1973-74	54.9	321.3
1977-78	51.3	328.9
1983	44.5	322.9
1987-88	38.9	307.1
1993-94	36	320.3
1999-00	26.1	263.3

Source: Planning Commission, Government of India.

For the first decades of planning in India- the 1950s, 60s and 70s–poverty in India stagnated at around 55%. These three decades were characterized by very low growth rates- the so called Hindu growth rate of 3.5%. This low growth rate, coupled with the population growth rate of 2.3% yielded a percapita income growth rate of a mere 1.2%. Naturally, this could not make any impact of on poverty. In the 1680's growth rate picked up to 5.6% due to initial internal liberalization .This improved growth rate brought down the poverty level of 38.9% by 1998 and 36% by 1994. Higher growth rate of around 6% in the post liberalization era further brought down the poverty ratio to 26% by 2000. The strong correlation between growth and poverty reduction is very clear.

Table 3
Distribution of people living on less than $1 a day Share of Population living on less than 1$ a day

Region	*Share of population*
South Asia	43.5%
Sub-Saharan Africa	24.3%
East Asia & Pacific	23.2%
Europe & Central Asia	2.0%
Latin America & the Caribbean	6.5%
Middle East & North Africa	0.5%

Source: World Development Report 2001.

In the millennium development goal of the U.N.D.P to halve the number of poor people is to be achieved by 2015, it will require drastic reduction of poverty in South Asia, Sub-Saharan Africa, East Asia and the Pacific.

POVERTY AND GROWTH

Recent experiences in poverty reduction points to a strong correlation between growth and poverty. The famous Columbian economist Xavier-Salai-Martin estimated poverty rates for 97 countries for the period 1970-98. His conclusion is that there is a strong correlation between growth and poverty reduction. Countries which grew fast like China, India and the Asian Tigers experienced drastic reduction in poverty. On the other hand, Africa experienced aggravation of poverty. The reason for this divergence was obvious: China, India and the Asian Tigers grew fast, Sub-Saharan Africa almost stagnated.

The case of India and China deserves special mention. One of the greatest reduction in poverty in history happened in the

1980s and 90s. Poverty declined in China from 28% in 1978 to 9% in 1998 (A.D.B. estimates). The drastic reduction that pulled millions out of poverty could be realized because China and India were among the five fastest growing economies of the world during this period with China in the lead. What happened in India and China happened in Vietnam and Uganda also: In Sub-Saharan Africa, poverty reduction happened in Botswana, Ghana, Mauritius and Uganda: the countries which experienced high rates of growth. In the rest of Sub-Saharan Africa poverty either stagnated or increased, because these regions experienced very low or no growth.

NEED FOR MULTY-PRONGED ATTACK ON POVERTY

Even though there is a strong correlation between growth and poverty reduction, drastic reduction and elimination pf poverty within the shortest possible time require a multy pronged attack on poverty. The elements of this strategy should include:

- Anti-poverty, employment generations programs.
- Increased public expenditure on primary education and public health.
- Empowerment of women to provide gender justice.
- Political empowerment of the voiceless and the powerless.
- Bringing the marginalized sections in to the mainstream.
- Improving market access to the marginalized.

Improving governance and greater democratization are central to the success of this strategy. Also, increasing state led programs will necessitate increasing public expenditure. Higher levels of public expenditure can be viably financed only by a buoyant economy. It is important to note that well meaning and ambitious public expenditure programs in an economy characterized by high fiscal deficit can have disastrous consequences. Anti-poverty strategies have to be framed keeping in mind.

The important principle that anti-poverty programs are palliatives, the lasting cure is growth.

REFERENCES

World Development Report 2000-2001, The Word Bank.

Word Development Report 2005, The Word Bank.

Human Development Report 2005, The UNDP.

Jadish, Bagvati (2004), In Defense of Globalization, Oxford University Press, New York.

Xavier Sala-i-Martin (2002), The World Distribution of Income Estimated from Individual Country Distributions, National Bureau of Economic Research W.P., Cambridge.

PART - VI
Tourism

B. VIJAYAKUMAR

Tourism and Information Technology in Kerala A Post Reform Scenario

10

INTRODUCTION

Tourism, the 20th century phenomenon, has been recognized as an engine of growth in terms of income, employment and foreign exchange by all national governments. Along with Information Technology, tourism plays a decisive role in the development paradigm of both developed and developing nations. Today tourism is seen as a form of modernization transferring capital; technology, expertise and modern values from the west to the less developed countries (Harison 1992). Literature and Statistics on the economic benefits of tourism shows that countries and destinations like Caribbean, Latin America, Australia, Spain, Britain, Switzerland, Mexico, USA, France, Maldives etc. derive substantial revenue from tourism. The World Tourism Organization has recorded that in 2002 the global tourist arrival is 702.6 million and excluding fare receipts, the World tourism receipts is 474.0 US $ billion (WTO, 2003). During the same period the share of India in tourist arrivals and receipt are 0.34 per cent and 0.62 per cent respectively signifying that the share of India in two cases remain less than one per cent (GOI, 2002). The global acceptance of tourism as an industry has brought planners, policy makers, environmentalist, technocrats, governments and non governmental organizations on a single plat from to chalk out programmes to develop tourism on sustainable lines. Simultaneously lured by this prospective industry, business corporations began to interfere in many aspects of this multifaceted industry.

The 'incredible India' as rightly popularized by the Department of tourism Government of India, had been a centre of attraction for foreigner's way back to several centuries. But the Government could make a policy pronouncement for tourism only in November 1982. An improvisation on this is found in the National Action Plan for tourism announced in May 1992. Between these two policy statements various legislative and executive measures were brought about. The report of the National Committee on Tourism submitted in 1988 need special mention. (Equation, 2000) Visible stress on Tourism development was given from VIII plan onwards. The New Economic Policy (1991) initiated by the government of India and the globalization process have given further impetus to tourism development in India. The provisional estimate (GOI, 2003) by Government of India shows that foreign tourist arrival is 2.75 million, registering 15.3% change over the previous year. During the same period, the foreign exchange earning is 3533 million $ US registering a change of 20.9% over the previous year. An over view of the programmes and projects on tourism over various plans (Planning Commission) shows that the central governments as well as the Department of tourism were giving more emphasis on infrastructure development particularly on accommodation. The Jha Committee (1963) also known as the Ad-hoc committee on Tourism recommended that the public sector should be given a leading role in tourism development. Accordingly in 1965, the GOI set up three public sector corporation namely, hotel Corporation of India Ltd., India Tourism Corporation Ltd., and India Tourism Transport undertaking Ltd. These Corporations were assigned the responsibility of construction and management of hotels in Public Sector, provision of publicity and transport. Later all these companies were merged and the India Tourism Development Corporation came into existence in 1970. Based on the recommendation of the Administrative Reform Commission, the control of Asoka Hotel Ltd., and the Janapath Hotels Ltd., was transferred to the Ministry of Tourism. Thus the dominance of Public Sector was the hall mark of tourism development in India in the initial period. But the new economic policy, and globalization have changed the course of state interference in tourism. Hotels began to be disinvested, to cite an example the disinvestment of ITDC at Kovalam, in Kerala-and the role of the government largely limited to a facilitator and not a key player in tourism industry. State control and regulations were minimized and private sector began to be promoted by new policy initiatives.

The role of transnational corporation in tourism has become prominent in 1980s. Hotels, airlines, and tour operation are the three segments of tourism industry, where transnational corporation placed greater emphasis (Lea 1988). After one and a half decade it is observed that these corporations have succeeded in establishing themselves in most of the developing economies particularly in the island economies. A good share of tourist expenditure is controlled by TNCs by handling hotels, airlines, and tour operations while the expenditure of the tourist at the destination on local transport, food and beverages and general shopping is highly minimized. By undertaking investment and selling franchise, the TNCs control most of the above said three segments of tourism industry and appropriate the profit there in. It has also been stated that equity investment, management contract, hotel leasing agreement, franchise agreement and technical service are the five major areas through which TNCs participate in the third world hotel industry.

Tourism and Information Technology are reckoned as sun rise sectors in the development paradigm of the state. Though both of them were in the world economic scenario, the development of the same in Kerala is a post reform phenomenon. Hence the policy initiative taken on both sectors were in line with the liberalization, privatization and globalization process. High level of literacy, proficiency in English, higher living standards, better adaptability and hospitality of the people make Kerala best suited for the development of Tourism and IT. In this context, an attempt is made to examine the role and potential of IT in the development of tourism in Kerala.

TOURISM ECONOMY OF KERALA

Notwithstanding the cultural heritage, communal harmony, diverse natural and cultural attractions, numerous festivals, traditional art, architecture and medicine, salubrious climate, educated and hospitable population, net work of transport and communication system, attempt to promote tourism in Kerala was made only in 1986 when it was given the status of an industry. The much awaited tourism policy of the state was announced in July 1995. At the outset, the policy accepted tourism as an economic activity of immense global importance. In the light of liberalization and globalisation, the policy is to serve as a guiding force to make maximum use of Kerala's tourism potential and also make it an ideal instrument for social and economic growth. The policy intended to promote a clear vision and provide direction for programmes to be organized in order to realize the growth of both domestic and international tourist substantially in the next five years. To attain this goal, the policy laid emphasis on the development of infrastructure, transport, human resource and marketing. Later in 2001, "To make Kerala, the Gods own country, an upmarket high quality tourist destination through rational utilization of resources with focus on integrated development of infrastructure sector, conserving and preserving the heritage and environment and enhancing productivity, income generating employment opportunities, alleviating poverty and there by making tourism the most important sector for the socio economic development and environment protection of the state, Government of Kerala have published a document called vision 2025 (Tourist statistics GOK 2001). There has been a consistent growth in the arrival of foreign tourists to Kerala since 1995 and the state has witnessed phenomenal growth in the earnings from tourism also.

The World Travel and Tourism Council in its Tourism Satellite Accounting Research Report States that, "Kerala is expected to register a record growth of 23.5% in the tourism sector over the next ten years. Kerala travel and tourism demand is expected to grow at a rate of 11.6% per annum over the coming decade registering highest record growth rate in the world tourism sector. The estimate on the economic benefit of tourism shows that an investment of US $110 million (2001-02) has taken place in the state, 6.29% of the SDP is contributed by tourism and the employment generated is 0.7 million". Considering the diverse natural attractions in the state and growing demand for nature based tourism internationally, the national geographic traveler identified Kerala as one of the 50 'must see destinations in one's life'. But mere presence of attractions will not make the industry competitive. The success of the industry depends mainly on how effectively it disseminates information to stake holders and get feed back especially from the tourists. Information Technology plays a decisive role in this context. Acknowledging that IT is in its infancy in the Tourism industry of Kerala, let us examines the possible role that IT can play in tourism especially in promoting and marketing.

Table 1
Growth of Foreign Tourist Arrivals and Earnings to Kerala (1995-2004)

Year	*Kerala (Nos)*	*Earnings (Rs. Crores)*	*% variation over previous year*
1995	142972	158.76	36.73
1996	176855	196.38	23.70
1997	182427	227.33	39.12
1998	189941	302.08	10.57
1999	202173	416.07	37.74
2000	209893	525.30	26.25
2001	208830	535.00	1.85
2002	232564	705.67	31.90
2003	294621	983.37	39.35
2004	345546	1266.77	28.82

Source: Dept. of Tourism, GOK.

TOURISM-AN INFORMATION BASED INDUSTRY

Tourism is a multifaceted industry drawing heavily from agriculture, small scale and cottage industries, transport, entertainment, hotel and restaurant etc. The products of the industry encompass attraction and amenities at the destination. Attractions may be natural or man made, where as amenities include accommodation, the services provided by hotel and restaurant, transport, entertainment etc. Unlike other products traded in the market tourism products commands certain special features. Neither the attraction, nor the amenities can be stored and marketed to places where the customer resides. As most of the tourism products are perishable, intangible and inseparable from the destination, the presence of the customer is inevitable where the product exist. This makes tourism products distinctive to other products traded in the market. More over one could not have a sample of tourism products to be tested before purchase is effected. This feature is more prominent in the services offered at the destination, especially those connected with hotels and restaurants, tour guides transport etc. The decision whether to buy a tourism product or not is taken on the basis of the information that the customer collects from various sources. To estimate the demand for various tourism products, the industry also is in need of information, which are available in tourism generating countries.

The major players in tourism industry are the tourists, travel agents, suppliers of other tourism services and tourism offices/government. The tourist need information about destination, facilities, availabilities, prices, border controls, exchange rates, geography, climate, risk factors etc. Tourists expect a 'second home' at the destination and hence all of the above exert considerable influence in setting the ambience to the visitor. The information needs of the travel agents who facilitate travel is centred around consumer's taste and preferences about destination facilities, availabilities, prices, border controls and tour packages. The suppliers of tourism products are more concerned about company information, about consumers, travel agents, tour operators and about competitors. Governments are interested in getting information about the size and nature of tourist flow, policies and plans for development. Out side this frame work, the NGOs and environmentalists would like to collect information on the potential impacts of tourism on socio-cultural economic and environmental fronts. (Pauline J. Sheldon 1999). The intricacies of information flows among government agencies, tourism organization, and association are well documented in a model by Pauline. Nevertheless, information is the cement that holds together the different producers with in the Travel and Tourism Industry. The links between and among tourism producers are provided not by goods but by the flow of information (Auliana Poon, 1998).

In the beginning information on destination are provided by word of mouth. Friends and relatives of travelers play a dominant role in this context. With the growth of tourism in an organized frame work the word of mouth is being supplemented by print media like brochures, journals, magazine, tour guides travel literature etc which again transcended to telephone and other communication media. The advent of information revolution and the availability of a net work of electronic devices have created a structural change in the mode of information provided to and by the industry.

INFORMATION TECHNOLOGY AND TOURISM

The information intensity of travel and tourism is a key driving force in the rapid diffusion of technology in the industry. No player in the tourism industry will be left untouched by information technology (Auliana Poon 1998). The rapid diffusion of technology in tourism is expected to improve the efficiency of production, improve the quality of services to visitors, generate new industry best practices. According to Auliana Poon while technology in old tourism is independent, less user friendly, slow to diffuse, single technology, limited use, distribution oriented, and more internally directed, the technology of new tourism is more integrated, user friendly rapid diffusion, system of technologies, all players are users, value oriented and global networking. The change in the use of technology between old and new tourism is conspicuous in areas like production, management, and marketing. Further the existence of a whole system of interrelated and communication technologies in new tourism have resulted in the creation of a System of Information Technologies (SIT). It encompasses teleconferencing, videos, video brochures, image communication, electronic fund transfer, computers, satellite communication, computerized reservation system (CRS) management information system, telephones, digital telephone network etc. The technology diffusion is expected to create its impacts on distribution and sales, management, service production and service delivery (Auliana Poon, 1998).

Consumer access to travel database is normally provided by the Internet and World Wide Web. The Internet and its protocol have created a universal platform for communication and presentation. It provides the consumers with the means to gain immediate access to relevant information of greater variety and depth than has been available previously. Travel Industry Association of America (TIA) research in 2001 has shown that a large majority of Internet using US travelers have bought air tickets and made hotel reservation on line (WTOBC, 2001). Consumer access is supplemented by Global Distribution System (GDS) Automatic Ticket Mechanism (ATM) Information Kiosk in public places, interactive TV, Videotext, Mobile devices, in-car technology etc. Computer accessibility and minimum level of computer literacy is expected from the customers to have easy access to information through these devices.

In the case of accommodation sector, Property Management System (PMS) is most important. The core function, of a hotel's information processing handled through a central computer, is called property management system. This will enable the hotels to disseminate and collect information in time and in a cost effective manner. The PMS interfaces covers central reservation system, call accounting system, electronic locking system, energy management system, self check in mechanism, credit card readers, point sale system, electronic refrigeration, guest room entertainments, voice messaging, and back office system. Hotels operating at international standards offer all these facilities where by timely information and security is provided to customers besides ensuring efficient management of their property (Pauline J. Sheldon 1999). A research study conducted by the Federation of Hotel and Restaurant Association of India (2003) on the use of IT in Indian hotels reveals that nearly all hotels in 5 star, 5 star deluxe categories have dial up internet facilities in the guest rooms. About 52% have high speed or broad band internet facility in the guest room. 41% of the remaining 5 star have plans to install this facility during the next one year. A number of information technology tools are used to assist industry players in producing services of different modes of transport, hotel bed nights packaged tours and information.

Marketing is one important areas where IT can make significant contribution in tourism. The tourists are very keen in getting latest/new information pertinent to the destination. Traditional devices like advertisement, brochures and video used for marketing destinations were replaced by CD Rom, Website, Internet etc. In most centres Government Tourism offices are responsible for managing and marketing destination. These offices maintain information centres that are manually operated at important cities/towns, railway stations, air ports etc to disseminate information on destination and quite often work as help desk to tourists. They rely heavily on printed brochures and verbal expertise to disseminate information. Though electronic media like World Wide Web and CD Rom have become popular, many countries are today using Destination Information System (DIS), to fill the gap left by other electronic media (Hanies P., 1994). Consumer web sites are widely used in tourism parlance by tourism generating countries.

THE KERALA SCENARIO

The Department of Tourism, Government of Kerala is the sole agency vested with the responsibility of promoting and marketing Kerala as a destination. With unique combination of winning tourism products, the state has always been a fascination for domestic as well as international tourists. Inbound tourist consider the state as a holistic destination for the mind, body and soul. Since tourism is considered as the most prospective sector in the development paradigm of the state, the economic achievements from tourism is largely influenced by the successful promotion and marketing of the destination. Till recently, the state have been following traditional mode of marketing like advertisement in national and international magazines, newspaper, brochures, fax, telephone etc. With the advent of information revolution the state switched over to CD Rom, Internet and website facilities. With a view to disseminate information and attracting more tourists to the state, today, besides E-mail (*deptour@vsnl.com*) the tourism department maintain a web site (*www. keralatourism.org*) and a toll free telephone (1600-444-747). Another major institution operating mainly in the accommodation sector under government control-the Kerala Tourism Development Corporation–maintain internet and offer on line booking facilities.

A pilot study conducted among seventeen major hotels ranging between 3 to 5 star in and around Trivandrum city on the use of information and communication technology reveals that invariably all of them have computerized accounting system. 71% of the hotels use computers for the front office management. Whereas only (24%) two five star, one four star and one three star hotels use computer facility in house keeping, 76% hotels have computer facility in the F & B sector and administration. However in stores 59% have computer facility. While 24% use self developed packages 53% make use of locally accepted versions like Hot Soft in their hotels.

Though the hotels in and around Trivandrum, the capital city of Kerala have started making use of information and communication technology for modernizing their business, they have to go a long way in this direction to accomplish the changing needs and requirements of modern tourist. In this regard a path breaking can be affected by initiating steps to promote and market Kerala as a destination by using Information Technology.

Given the back drop that Government of Kerala has recognized tourism and information technology as prospective sectors in the state's economy and the synergy of IT with tourism, an attempt was made to collect expert opinion to explore further possible areas where IT can be effectively used to promote and market Kerala as a tourism destination. The experts participated in the Delphi study include tourism professionals, administrators and IT professionals. The aim of the Delphi study was to arrive on consensus among experts on various aspects related to the application of IT in marketing tourism. Thirty six experts initially participated in the first round and in the following round twenty five experts responded promptly. Seventeen statements pertaining to the use of IT in tourism marketing were placed before experts and they were asked to respond on this by using seven scale rating– Strongly agree (1) Moderately agree (2) Agree (3) No comment (4) Disagree (5) Moderately disagree (6) Strongly disagree (7)- of which one is regarded as most acceptable and seven is to be rejected absolutely. In between these the degree of opinion varies. The individual expert opinion collected is used for getting a statistical group response. The forecast made by the group will tell us the majority's view point on the issue. The statistical response presented by the Delphi procedure includes the opinion of the entire panel on a single question. The group response is presented in terms of three quartiles, the second quartile median being the average opinion of the experts. Thus each opinion within the group is taken into account in the median and the spread of opinion is shown by semi inter quartile range. In most Delphi, consensus is assumed to have been achieved when a certain percentage of votes fall within a prescribed range. In this study where Q3-Q1/2 is less than or equal to one is taken as consensus. Statements on which consensus have not been arrived during the first round of the study were placed before the expert in the second round after incorporating the suggestion received in the first round. The final result of the Delphi study is given in Table 2.

DISCUSSION

Infrastructure in terms of human resource, telecommunication system, computers etc. greatly influence the application of IT in productive services. With cent per cent literacy, spread of higher education, good working knowledge in English,

Table 2
Delphi Results

Sl. No.	*Statements*	*Q2*	*Q3*	*Q1*	*QD*
1.	Technically skilled man power and good network of telecommunication system are positive factors for promoting IT in Kerala.	1	1	1	0
2.	Higher education and spread of English language in Kerala can immensify help the growth of IT enabled services	1	2	1	.5
3.	The use of personal computer is fast spreading in Kerala which in turn can facilitate the growth of IT industry.	1	2	1	.5
4.	Timely and accurate information relevant to the consumer need is the key to satisfaction of tourist demand	1	2	1	.5
5.	It is always not possible to give minute details on destination in websites.	3	5	3	1
6.	To improve the accessibility, accuracy, comprehensiveness, timeliness, quality of information, a Destination Information System (DIS) may be established in Kerala.	2	3	1	1
7.	Local information system may be launched at Calicut and Ernakulam to collect detailed information on visitors, attractions, and facilities locally that may be linked to DIS.	2	3	1	1
8.	The service of DTPC may be used to collect local information in detail including availability of facility, tariff change etc to supplement the LIS.	3	3	2	.5
9.	DIS can fill the gap left by the Global Distribution System (GDS)	3	4	2	1
10.	Pre trip and post arrival information requirement from the marketing offices in foreign country/information centre in Kerala can be handled by the DIS.	3	3	2	.5
11.	DIS can create database of the customers (demographic, travel preferences etc) for preparing marketing strategy.	2	3	1	1
12.	The data may be sold to needy supplier of tourism service.	3	3	1	1
13.	Customer database can be used to encourage repeat visitors to destination	2	3	1	1

Sl. No.	*Statements*	*Q2*	*Q3*	*Q1*	*QD*
14.	With DIS, information on forth coming events or promotion can be marketed to visitors of particular interest.	2	3	1	1
15.	CD Rom can be used in the place of videos film and brochures to get better results.	2	3	1	1
16.	The use of internet can increase the number of online customers	1	2	1	.5
17.	The use of IT in air lines hotels and travel agencies can promote better property management system and management of information to meet their requirement of operational and strategic decision.	1	2	1	.5

availability of IT professionals both hardware and software, Kerala offer quality human resource for promoting IT enabled services in the state. The state has a modern telecom network comprises of digital switches inter connected by optical fibre/ microwave/satellite media. The state is served by 1207 automatic exchanges which are digital electronic. The total equipped capacity including WLL is 45.16 lakh lines and the number of telephone connection working including WLL is 36.50 lakh. The telephone density of the state is 114.3 per thousand populations and rural telephone density is 100 per thousand populations. Kerala circle plans to provide 6.55 lakh connections in the basic telecom net work during 2006-07. The circle has the 2nd largest net work out of 24 territorial circles in the century. As on 30.09.2005 there are 8 33060 mobile and approximately 2.5 lakhs internet connection in the state. The communication sector in the state is further strengthened of private agencies like Idea, BPL, Reliance, Tata etc. (Economic Review 2002). Experts strongly agree on the first three statements that the availability of technically skilled manpower, network of communication facilities and higher education are factors that can provide conducive environment for the growth of IT enabled services in Kerala. Tourism, an information based industry can make markable progress provided these facilities are exploited for the application of IT in tourism. Further experts strongly agree that timely and accurate information relevant to the consumer's need is the key to satisfaction of tourist demand (Statement No. 4). Quite often destinations at far off places are strange to tourist. Hence tourists, particularly long haul tourist, are very particular in getting latest information on facilities, climate environment etc. Timely and reliable information will equip them to accommodate themselves with changes, if any, at the destination. In this regard IT can be used for better information dissemination to customers.

Most of the destinations today possess their web sites giving their information. Searching web sites have become a common practice among, tourist particularly from the developing part of the world. Experts agree that it is always not possible to give minute details of destination in web sites (statement No. 5). However this is not the fault of IT but the way in which information upgradation is made is important. This is prominent in less developed part of the world where once web site is launched very little attention is given for constant upgradation of information. Since tourism is a multi faceted industry and stakeholders are many, changes taking place in any one of the spheres can upset the calculation of tourist. Provided web sites are not upgraded by incorporating latest and minute information, the purpose will not be served.

In order to fill the gap left by other electronic media many tourism departments are creating Destination Information System (DISs). This electronic database of destination facilities is of immense use to travelers. It improves the accessibility, accuracy comprehensiveness, and quality of information to tourist. Experts moderately agree on this (Statement No. 6) and suggest that the Department of Tourism, Government of Kerala can take the lead to establish a destination information system. The use of DIS terminals isimportant in tourism information centres and marketing offices abroad improve the efficiency of information distribution on many lines. It can also be accessed over the World Wide Webb if designed properly. The DIS may also have a reservation capability for accommodation and other facilities in the destination (Wayne, 1991).

Constant upgradation of DIS in Kerala context is possible by taking steps to collect accurate information locally. Besides Trivandrum, Ernakulam and Calicut are two major points of arrivals to both national and international tourists. While Ernakulam is centrally located, Calicut is the focal point of the northern Kerala. Local Information Systems at Ernakulam and Calicut can collect information relating to local programmes, daily changes in tariff, availability of facilities, and profile of tourist and can supplement the DIS. While experts moderately agree on this (statement No. 7), they agree that the District. Tourism, Promotion Council can collect and transfer minute tourist details pertaining to their district to the local information system (Statement No. 8). A good number of natural and cultural attractions, however small it may be, lie hidden in various parts of the state. The DTPCs can identify this and make significant contribution to LIS, which in turn enrich the DIS. They also agree that the DIS can fill the gap, if any left by the Global Distribution System. GDSs tend to favour large chain companies with high price product. Low cost, accommodation and out door activities are normally excluded in GDS. Irrespective of large or small, high or low cost, DIS include all types of facilities and activities and there by fill the gap left by GDS (Statement No. 9).

Pre trip and post arrival information are of immense use for formulating suitable marketing strategy for tourism products. The information requirements of pre trip by the tourists are basically different from that of post arrival. This information can be collected from marketing offices in foreign countries and information centres in Kerala and can be handled by the DIS. As experts agree on this consensus have been arrived with an inter quartile range .5 (Statement 10).

Concrete database of customers is another important area (Statement No.11) that facilitate the formation of suitable marketing strategy. Information on the profile of tourists, and their travel preferences will help us to segment tourist and appropriate marketing strategies can be framed. DIS can be used to collect the database of visitors and the same can be analysed to frame suitable marketing strategies. This database can be used for promoting direct marketing also. Considering this fact experts moderately agree this and consensus is reached on this.

Maintaining DIS is not a cost less affair. Though the department of tourism can facilitate the promotion and marketing of tourism in general, the database collected by the DIS may be used to generate some income to the department. Experts agree that the data may be sold to needy suppliers of tourism products (statement No. 12). Initially, the suppliers may not be interested in the database of DIS. But if the DIS can generate detailed database of tourist and proved beyond doubt that through segmenting the market more tourist can be attracted, suppliers will use the data base to encourage repeat visitors to Kerala. Experts moderately agree on this (statement No. 13). The climate, art forms, backwaters, ayurvedic therapy are the most important factors that promote repeat visit to Kerala. A data base on this will enable the state to enter into direct marketing with out video, and brochures. Further information on forthcoming events like Thrisoor Pooram, Sabari Mala festivals', boat races Nisagandhi dance festival, Food festivals etc. can be marketed to visitors of particular interest. Experts moderately agree to this (Statement No. 14). They also moderately agree that CD Rom can be used in the place of videotext and brochures for effective marketing (Statement No. 15). In this context it may be noted that the Department of Tourism use CD Romes for marketing the diverse tourism attraction of the state, more focus on this will bring better results in this direction.

On issues like use of Internet and IT in air lines and hotels experts strongly agree that heavy reliance should be given to the application of IT. While Internet can facilitate on line booking (Statement No. 16), IT in airlines hotel and travel agencies can be used for better property management system, improved efficiency and reduce cost (Statement No. 17). Hence from the operational point of view, application of IT can help the tourism industry to frame appropriate marketing strategies to attract more tourist and make tourism a round the year phenomenon–no off season-in this Gods Own Country.

CONCLUSION

Product development and marketing are two important components of successful tourism business. Kerala has already developed a good variety of tourism products and now it is high time to focus on sound marketing strategies where technology can play a decisive role. The department of tourism, suppliers of services and the tourists are in need of timely accurate and comprehensive information. A destination information system under the aegis of the Department of tourism, besides maintaining credibility can serve the dual purpose of information gathering and dissemination. By making use of the existing network of institutions the department can collect authentic information about on going activities, 'unseen Kerala' and offer quality service to the tourist. If the information is found to be false, there is the danger of the entire DIS losing its credibility. Besides the date base on tourists can be used to promote market research and forecasting, which will have a strong bearing in framing suitable marketing strategy for future. The sound infrastructure in telecommunication sector is an added advantage for Kerala to use IT for sales and marketing of accommodation, travel and tour operations. The policy initiatives of the State Government on Tourism and IT are based on new economic policy. Today, private sector plays a dominant role in these areas. Being a facilitator, the state government promotes both sectors, for better integration with national and international economies. However, it may be noted that under the decentralized frame work, efforts are also being under taken to promote community involvement in tourism and IT. The IT@school, Akshaya, Thenmala Ecotourism and Tourism at Kumarakom etc. stand testimony to this.

NOTES

Some important Web sites (WTO) in E-Business for tourism is given. Besides attractions these sites provide information on facilities and availabilities.

Canadian Tourism Commission (CTC)–http://www.travelcanada.ca

German National Tourist Board (GNTB)-http://www.germany_tourism.de.

Egyptian Tourist Authority-http://www.touregypt.net.

Japan National Tourist Organisation (JNTO)-http://www.jnto.go.jp

Tourism Malaysia-http://www.tourism.gov.my

Mexico Ministry of Tourism-http://www.mexico_travel.com

Turespana-http://www.tourspain.es

Switzerland Tourism-http://www.myswitzerland.com

Tourism Authority of Thailand: //www.tourismthailand.org

British Tourist Authority (BTA) US Gateway-http://www.visitbritain.com

Edinburgh & Lothians Tourist Board-http://www.edinburgh.org.

New York State Division of Tourism-http://www.iloveny.com.

Ontario Travel, Travelinx-http://www.travelinx.com

Commonwealth of Pennsylvania, '100% Pennsylvania Experience-http://www.experiencepa.com

Azienda Per la promozione Turistica del Trentino-http://www.trentino.to

Wallonie Bruxelles office de promotion du Tourisme-http://www.belgium_tourism.net

Turisme de Barcelona-http://www.barcelonaturisme.com

Budepest Tourism Office-http://www.budapestinto.liu

Canberra Tourism and Events Corporation-http://www.Canberratourism.cam.au

Wonderful Copenhagen-http://www.visit copenhagen.dk

London Tourist Board-http://www.londontown.com

Paris Convention and Visitors Bureau-http://www.paris_touristoffice.com

Vienna Tourist Board-http://info.wien.at

Zurich Tourism-http://www.zurichtourism.ch

REFERENCES

Auliana Poon (1998), *Tourism, Technology and Competitive Strategies*, CABI International, UK.

Equations, Bangalore, Tourism Policy, Critical Review, 1998.

Federation of Hotel and Restaurant Association of India (2003), *A Research Study on Use of information Technology in Indian Hotels.*

Government of Kerala (1995), *Tourism Policy.*

Government of Kerala (2001), *Tourist Statistics.*

Government of Kerala (2001), *Vision 2025.*

Government of Kerala (2005), *Economic Review.*

Government of India (2002), *National Tourism Policy.*

Hanies, P. (1994), Destination Marketing System. In: *Information and Communication Technologies in Tourism,* Proceedings of International Conference on Information and Communication Technologies in Tourism, New York.

Harrison, D. (1992), *International Tourism and the Less Developed Countries,* John Wiley and Sons, UK.

Pauline J. Sheldon (1999), *Tourism Information Technology,* CBAI International, UK.

Wayne, N. (1991), *A Case Study of Working Computerized Central Reservation Office in the Public Sector Tourism;* Proceedings of Information Technology in Public Tourism Offices Conference, Assisi, Italy.

World Tourism Organization (2001), *E-Business For Tourism–Practical Guide lines for Tourism Destinations and Business.*

World Tourism Organization, 2002.

PART - VII

Tribal Economy

SEETHA KAKKOTH

Tribal Economy: Reforms & Unequal Partners

11

INTRODUCTION

The Structural Adjustment Programmes (SAP), differently named as the economic reconstruction programmes, new economic policy, economic adjustment programmes etc., have implemented during 1990s, as a part of IMF and World Bank, for liberalizing the markets and creating an environment for global transfer of goods, services, capital and labour to meet the needs of global capitalism. These progrmmes have affected almost all sections of Indian economy and our forest wealth is not an exception.

Indian forests are richly endowed with natural resources like timber, bamboo, medicinal plants, non-wood forest products (n.w.f.p), water, mineral wealth etc., and it is the abode of many tribes, whose dependence on forest ecosystem is found to be total. But their livelihood is ignored by colonial and later by post-colonial rulers in extracting timber and other forest products and still later by the current global-cum-national environmental system for increasing supply of needed global environmental goods. Several World Bank funded projects have already deteriorated the condition of the forests and forest dwelling communities (George, 2004). State management of forests has neither preserved natural capital nor provided adequate livelihood sources for the indigenous people dependent on forests (Nathan & Kelkar; 2004: 15).

It is a fact that majority of the activities for the economic development of the country are undertaken in the forest ecosystem and in many cases though the tribes bear the cost of socio-economic development activities, the benefits are largely cornered by non-tribes. Moreover, the forest depended tribal communities are forced to change their livelihood pattern from a system based on stability, reciprocity and subsistence to one based on accumulation. The forest based tribal economy in most parts of the world is women based (Geetha Menon: 1987, 1991). Hence, any change in the forest ecosystem affects the tribal community in general and that of their womenfolk in particular.

Anthropological studies have shown that when simple indigenous societies were forced to change from their subsistence based economy to new economic activities due to the impact of market economy and globalisation, adjustments occurred not only in their traditional livelihood pursuits but in their social institutions as well. Switch over to a monetised economy often resulted in discontinuance of traditional subsistence practices. Vital social institutions of simple societies which are closely linked to and centred around their traditional subsistence activities lost their economic importance significantly due to shift in occupations. In such situations, they continued to exist mainly as a cultural phenomenon (Sathyanarayanan: 2003). For the indigenous communities like the Adivasis and Dalits, their dependency on land and forest is not just as a productive asset but as a symbol of their self-determination, co-existence, community feeling and dignity. Now this became a tradable commodity (George, 2004).

In this context, an attempt is made to examine the impact of market economy, development programmes and related issues on the traditional livelihood pattern, social institutions and role of gender among the Aranadan. Usual anthropological methods like interview, observation (both participant & non-participant) and schedules were employed for the data collection.

II

ARANADAN

Aranadan is one among the 36 Scheduled Tribes of Kerala and are seen distributed in the marginal areas of forests coming under Karulai and Kalikavu ranges of Nilambur south forest division and Vazhikadavu range of Nilambur north forest division. The Nilambur forests, which stretch an area of 760.29 sq. km, are covered largely by semi-deciduous and wet evergreen forests. The Valley has an elevation ranging between 40m and 250m above MSL. The Valley is characterized by heavy rainfall, humid climate, moderate temperature and is rich with varied flora and fauna.

Aranadan is considered to be the autochthonous tribe of Erand taluk and also known as Ernadan, meaning, people of Ernad (Thurston: 1909, Luiz: 1962). Their population Contains 254 persons consisting of 128 males and 126 females (Survey: 1995). The sex ratio is 984 females per thousand males and the average family size is 4.03. The number of couples at the time of survey was 56. The population below the age of 14 constitutes only 22.45 per cent and that of female population is 10.6. This shows that the population has a shrunk base. Literacy rate among the Aranadan is only 21.26 per cent.

Nuclear family is the basic socio-economic unit of the Aranadan. They are patrilineal and patrilocal/neolocal. The community is politically acephalous. But at hamlet-level, eldest male member, called *chemmakkaran,* functions as their socio-political and religious head. The Aranadan are monogamous and follow different types of marriage include cross cousin, parallel cousin, levirate, sororate, marriage by exchange etc. Bride price is prevalent. Aranadan are animist and burry the dead.

III

SUBSISTENCE PATTERN & ROLE OF GENDER : PAST

In the early part of the 20th century, the Aranadan were leading a semi-nomadic life in the lower valley of Nilambur forests. Earlier writers report that Aranadan used strapped plantain leaves or *malmpunna* (Dillenia bracteata) leaves to cover their body (Thurston: 1909., Luiz: 1962). Their traditional dwelling is temporary shed like structure called *pandal* or *pira,* made of wild twigs, jungle poles and thatched with reed or teak leaves.

The traditional subsistence pattern of the Aranadan was based on food gathering - small scale hunting, fishing, and the collection non-wood forest produces. Their collection pursuits are confined to semi-deciduous forests of the lower valley and fringes of the forests. Usually both husband and wife proceeded together to the forests in the morning, for the collection of various forest produce such as roots, tubers, leaves, fruits, mushrooms etc., and return to their *pira* in the evening with gathered items and shared with the family members. The commonly collected roots and tubers include *noora, nagavalli, kavala, panchiputta, korana, pathivenni, mooval, padakizhangu, mookuchuve* etc. Very simple implements like *kottu* and *choorakathi* are used for food gathering and some of these tubers are eaten on the spot by fire-roasting. Gathering was done around the year. But during lean periods (i.e., from June to August/September) they collect variety of edible mushrooms for self-consumption.

Their hunting is limited to small games like tortoise, crab etc. They also hunt python. Among the tribes if Nilambur Valley, the Aranadan is the only tribe who eat the flesh of python. Both husband and wife participate in python hunting. After a hunt, they bring it to the hamlet, cut into several pieces using hand axe and the flesh is shared among them.

They usually do fishing during summer, using bunding and bailing out techniques or by using some stupefying plant matters. Collection of n.w.f.p is another activity during summer. *Thenu* (Apies sp), *thenmezhuku* (honey wax.), *cheenikka* (Acacia concinna), *kurumulaku* (Piper nigrum), *marottikuru* (Hydnocarpus pentandra), *mullilakkay* (Zanthoxylum rhetsa), *nellikka* (Phyllanthus emblica), *maramanjal* (Coscinium fenestratum), *kanchirakkuru* (Strychnos nux-vomica) etc are the main n.w.f.p collected by the Aranadan from the semi-deciduous forests. They exchanged these items with forest contractors for rice and condiments.

Thus, it is seen that, in the past, both Aranadan males and females followed almost similar economic activities. For them, small scale hunting and food gathering were primary and the collection of n.w.f.p, fire-wood and medicinal plants were secondary. Moreover, bountiful nature of Nilambur forests provided varieties resources, which helped the community to fulfill their nutritional requirements in the past. Moreover, their economy was characterized by reciprocity and self-sufficiency. Earlier they had very little contacts with the non-tribes and that too were limited to the transaction of forests products. Their intensity of interaction with outsiders increased owing to the monetisation of their livelihood as a result of the various development activities in the area.

IV

DEVELOPMENT ACTIVITIES & MONETISATION OF THE ARANADAN LIVELIHOOD

The commercialization of forest produces has started during the colonial period. The British started the first ever teak plantation in the world at Nilambur in 1882. Nilambur was connected to Shoranur by a meter gauge rail-road in 1927 by the British to transport timber. The Forest Department also had its own working plan for the exploitation of the forests of the area. During 1970-85, thousands of acres of semi-deciduous forests have been converted into teak and rubber plantations. Teak plantation activities have become intense in the last thirty years. The Karulai Forest Range (covering an area of 265.608 sq. km.), where majority of the Aranadan do foraging, was converted to teak plantation. The planting of teak trees also requires the bringing in of non-tribal labourers in good number. In teak plantations, every four years there is thinning and logging activities, for which the non-tribes are deployed. It is also observed that after felling the forests, the area is given for cultivating various dry land crops. These cultivations are undertaken by the non-tribes. Thus, within the last forty years, non-tribal population influx has been taking place in the region and several growth centres have sprung up near the forests owing to settler influx.

In 1970's and 1980's the Government established colonies and the Aranadan were rehabilitated in these colonies. The distance from these colonies to the forests varies from 1 km to 5km. All these colonies are located on the marginal areas of rural habitations and accessible by jeep. Recently, road communication has improved greatly in the area.

In 1976, a Co-operative Society viz., Kalkulam Girijan Service Co-operative Society (currently known as Nilambur Pattikavarga Vikasana Society) was formed for the transaction of n.w.f.p collected by the tribal communities of the area. An Integrated Tribal Development Project (ITDP) area has been carved out in 1983 with Nilambur as its head quarters. ITDP has implemented various schemes such as housing, drinking water, digging trenches around forest hamlets for protection from wildlife etc.

It is estimated in 1994-95 that the forests of Kerala covers 28.88% of the total geographical area. The report of the National Ramote-sensing Agency (NRA) shows a reduction of forests of the Western Ghats from 20 per cent (during 1950s) to 11.25 per cent by 2000. The Nilambur forest where the Aranadan inhabit is also a part of Western Ghats. Recently, Participatory Forest Management programme (PFM) was also implemented in this area by the Forest Department, in order to protect, manage and regenerate the NTFP (Non-Timber Forest Products) items with the active participation of forest dependent communities.

It is observed that during the last forty years or so, the Nilambur Valley had experienced tremendous modifications. Large tracts of the forests of the Valley had been converted into teak and rubber plantations, resulting deforestation and the depletion of natural resources in which the Aranadan depend for their livelihood. Though foraging is in practice among the Aranadan since long, this pattern has changed in recent times owing to various reasons like depletion of resources, alien-culture contact, settler influx, market pressures etc.

V

SUBSISTENCE PATTERN & ROLE OF GENDER : PRESENT

At present, the economic pursuits vary from family to family. Collection of various n.w.f.p is the major activity for both males and females during summer. These items are exchanged with the Tribal Co-operative Society (TCS) of the area for cash, rice, condiments, utensils, implements etc. N.w.f.p items collected by the TCS, the rate given to tribes and price obtained from sale are shown in Table 1.

Works like loading and unloading of timber, boundary clearing, bamboo cutting, weed clearance in teak plantation, teak seed collection fire-wood etc., are other labour avenues. These works are seasonal and the Aranadan are employed only when there occur shortage of non-tribal labourers. Among the work force of the area, the Aranadan is considered as having poor work habits and hence they are least preferred. Here also the Aranadan remains unequal in the eyes of Forest Department too.

During the rainy season, Aranadan men work as agricultural labourers in the fields of the neighbouring communities. For this, they are paid Rs. 120/- or above a day. They are also given mid-day meal and tea. They work along with non-tribals like Kalladi, Cheruman, Kanakkan etc. Recently, Aranadan youths are found attracted to coconut plucking. Coconut plucking is a part-time labour and well paid by owners. This is an emerging opportunity, which stem from traditional skill in tree climbing.

Table 1
NWFP Item Collected by TCS & Price/kg

Sl. No.	*Name of NWFP*	*Appro. price/kg (to Tribes)*	*Appro. price/kg (Sale to Outsiders)*
1.	Thenu (honey)	Rs. 55/-	Rs. 85/-
2.	Cheruthen	Rs. 100/-	Rs. 140/-
3.	Thenmezhuku	Rs. 80/-	Rs. 170/-
4.	Cheenikka	Rs. 8/-	Rs. 12/-
5.	Marottikuru	Rs. 20/-	Rs. 30/-
6.	Mullilakkay	Rs. 12/-	Rs. 15/-
7.	Nellikka*	(directly given to outsiders Rs.10/-)	
8.	Padakizhangu	Rs. 45/-	Rs. 70/-
9.	Maramanjal	Rs. 10/-	Rs. 20/-
10.	Kollakai	Rs. 10/-	Rs. 12/-
11.	Kakkumkai	Rs. 3/-	Rs. 6/-
12.	Kodampuli	Rs. 30/-	Rs. 45/-
13.	Manjakoova	Rs. 18/-	Rs. 25/-

(Primary Data: November, 2005)
*Items, which are not taken by the Tribal co-operative society.

As far as Aranadan females are concerned, along with n.w.f.p, the collection of medicinal plants and fire-wood form their major economic activities. Their secondary economic activities include food gathering, weed clearance in teak plantation, teak seed collection. Gathering of medicinal plants for commercial trade is a recent phenomenon and almost 90% females are now engaged in this activity, especially during rainy season. They roam the lower valley semi-deciduous forests, covered by monoculture teak plantation, riverine forest patches, bamboo and reed thickets from dawn to dusk with empty stomach and collect various medicinal plants like *amalpori* (Rauvolfia serpentina), *incha* (Acacia caesia), *idampiri valampiri* (Helicteres isora), *maramanjal* (Coscinuim fenestratum), *koduveli* (Plumbago indica), *kurunthotti,* (Sida retusa), *moovila* (Psuedarthria viscida), *sathavari* (Asparagus racemosus), *nannari* (Hemidesmus indicus), *pambuvalli* (Sida rhombifolia), *padakizhangu* (Cyclea peltata), *orila* (Desmodium gangeticum) and *thippali* (Piper longum). The medicinal plants thus collected are transacted with the agents of private ayurveda pharmaceutical companies for very meagre amount, as the Tribal Co-operative Society is not keen in the collection of these items. (Now, TCS collects certain selected items like *maramanjal padakizhangu, amalpori* and *orila*). It is observed that after a whole day's tedious work (roaming vast areas, spending more energy and time), they earn only Rs.10 to 30 from these dealings. The local traders thus act as agents of markets, utilise the traditional knowledge of the Aranadan and procure medicinal plants for meager amount.

The Aranadan women are also less paid or unpaid or under paid in the case of the transaction of fire-wood too. They take firewood collected to growth centers where tea shops are in good number or to non-tribal households. For a bundle of fire-wood, Aranadan men get Rs. 40/- where as women are paid only Rs. 20/-. In the cases of wage labour and plantation work also women are underpaid. (See Table 2).

Table 2
Economic Activities & Wages given

Economic Activities	*Wages*	*Male Female*
Wage labour	Rs. 120/day	Rs. 60/day
Plantation work	Rs. 80/day	Rs. 50/day
Fire-wood	Rs. 40/bundle	Rs. 20/bundle
Coconut plucking	Rs. 140/day	–(Appro.)
Medicinal plants	–	Rs. 10- 30/day *(Appro.* *(wages vary acc. to items)*

(Primary Data: December, 2004)

ANALYSIS

Economic Activities: Past & Present

As mentioned, the subsistence pattern of the Aranadan is greatly influenced by various factors like plantation activities, deforestation, alien-culture contact, depletion of forest resources, market pressures etc. A comparative analysis of the economic activities of the Aranadan (Table 3) past and present showed a shift of their prime economic activity from hunting and food gathering to n.w.f.p collection.

Table 3
Economic activities-Past & Present

	Past		Present	
	Male	Female	Male	Female
Primary	hunting (small games) Food gathering	hunting (small games) Food gathering	n.w.f.p forest labour wage labour	n.w.f.p medicinal plants Fire-wood Fishing
Secondary	n.w.f.p Fishing medicinal plants	n.w.f.p Fire-wood Fire-wood	coconut plucking hunting (small games) hunting (small games)	plantation work Fishing Food gathering

For males, in addition to n.w.f.p collection, forest labour and wage labour form their primary economic activity and hunting become secondary. In the case of females, along with n.w.f.p, collection of medicinal plants and fire-wood has become the major activity. Thus, a clear-cut division of labour in accordance with sex is observed in the present economic scenario, which was insignificant in their traditional economy.

The commercialization of forest resources has led to the introduction of cash economy in the life of Aranadan, slowly replacing their traditional self-sufficient subsistence pattern and eroding the ecological equilibrium the tribe has established with their immediate environment. Habitat destruction and commercialization have forced the Aranadan youths to discard their traditional way of life and adapt to the changing situations. So they have become commercial n.w.f.p collectors, wage labourers and a few have become coconut pluckers. Thus, markets play a major role in the transformation of their livelihood strategies and options. Changes in the economic pattern also had its reflection on the social life of the community.

VI

Present Economy, Society & Gender: Impact

It has already been stated elsewhere that the Aranadan are monogamous with low population size and low female sex ratio. Traditionally, in a monogamous family, both husband and wife engaged in same economic activities within the forest ecosystem and shared the burden of running the family. But, this traditional livelihood pattern had transformed into a monetised economy owing to various development activities in the area.

Now, there is a shift from kinship-based collectivity for subsistence to a cizitenship-based collectivity for accumulation and the Aranadan have become part and parcel of the market network. Majority of male members at present are engaged in n.w.f.p collection, forest labour and wage labour under non-tribes. But females still do their economic pursuits within the lower valley forests and are less paid or unpaid or under paid when compared to males. Lion share of the money earned are spend for alcohol, smoking and chewing and women are not exceptions. This often leads to frequent quarrel within the families and later leads to its breakdown. Being an acephalous political organisation, nobody stands as mediator. Among the population of 254 persons, there exist 14 female divorcees and 8 male divorcees. The female divorcee per 1000 population comes to 55.12. It reveals that the Aranadan marriages are very weak and unstable. In broken families children live with their mother. So usually, the burden of running the families false on the shoulder of females.

Usually females go for collection pursuit in the morning without taking any food as there will be seldom food at their home. If there is previous day's left over food, it is given to children or male members. The collection of medicinal plants and fire wood consumes more time and energy and usually females spend the whole day in the forests with empty stomach. But the case of their men is different. 80% of them are now wage labourers or forest labourers. Usually they are given food by their employers in the morning and noon. So they will not starve during day-time. Thus, when compared to men, the health status of the Aranadan women is very weak. Sen started writing about the role of women in development early in 1960s "It seemed to me that the gender inequality were manifest in every aspect. When I was looking at the pattern of hunger or of schooling and at such matters as the allocation of resources within the family, the inequalities seemed so apparent that I was surprised that people didn't talk about it" (in Kunhaman, 2002). This observation is still relevant and applicable not only to the Aranadan but to the Indian situation as well.

The colonization of Aranadan in the midst of rural population accelerated their contact with the outsiders and market. This contact often resulted in the exploitation of the Aranadan females by contactors and non-Aranadan co-workers. Non-Aranadan sometimes establishes marital alliances with Aranadan women. But these relationships too are fragile and in majority cases, Aranadan females are deserted by their non-Aranadan husbands, after few months.

Thus, it is observed that the operation of market force is very significant in the Nilambur area and the Aranadan are also occupying a place in the market network. In order to adapt with the changing situation, they have lost many of their life supporting systems like the loss of biodiversity, loss of their local traditional knowledge, loss of their traditional occupational skills and many more. All this losses are directly linked to the transformation of the original landscape and level market linkages.

VII

CONCLUSION

Reforms are a means to achieve the ultimate goal of economic development of the country and the well-being of its people. According to 1998 World Bank Report on India "Reform is not needed for its own sake but for the sake of India's poor both in the interest of having them contribute to the growth process and having them benefit from it" (Nagesh Kumar, 2000). It is seen that India's forest resources have contributed much to the growth process, but instead of getting benefits from it, forest dependent tribes in general and that of their womenfolk in particular pay much for it. "Among the indigenous people, the destruction of indigenous welfare system of reciprocity and the rupture of access to productive resources, push destitute women, with their continuing responsibilities for household food security, into selling their bodies for sexual services" (Nathan & Kelkar; 2004: 292). This negative effect of the development of market relations is applicable to the Aranadan community also.

In short, changes in the immediate ecosystem in the form of plantation activities, deforestation, non-tribal influx and acculturation, under the folder of 'economic development' of the country, had a negative impact not only on the livelihood pattern of this tribal community but the entire social institutions as well. The transition from subsistence economy to market economy has resulted in gender inequality in division of labour and gender bias in access to food and resources. Depletion of natural resources and degradation of environment have a direct bearing on the time and energies of women. Their work is unseen and are exploited by officials, contractors and non-tribal immigrants. Thus, it is disappointed to note that any reform with a goal of economic development of the country and the well-being of its people has failed (among other things) to recognize the burden of marginalized sections like women, especially, tribal women and are still treated as unequal partners in enjoying the benefit of development. .

REFERENCES

Dash, Dhanlaxmi (2005), *Women Environment and Health.* Jaipur: Mangal Deep Publications.

George, Goldy M. (2004), 'Free Trade-A War Against Dalits & Adivasis'. *Countercurrents.org.*

Kakkoth, Seetha (2001), Three Tribes of Nilambur Valley: A Study in Interrelationship between Habitat, Economy, Society and Culture, Unpublished Ph.D. thesis submitted to the University of Calicut, Kerala.

Kunhaman, M.K. (2002), *Globalisation: A Subaltern Perspective.* Thiruvananthapuram: Centre for Subaltern Studies.

Luiz, A.A.D. (1962), *Tribes of Kerala.* Bharatiya New Delhi: Adimjati Sevak Sangh.

Menon, Geetha (1991), 'Ecological Transitions and the Changing Context of Women's in Tribal India'. *Purushartha,* 14, pp. 291-314.

Menon,Geetha (1987), 'Tribal Women: Victims of Development Process'. *Social Action,* Vol. 37.

Nagesh Kumar (2000), 'Economic Reforms and their Macroeconomic Impact', *Economic and Political Weekly,* Vol. 35, No. 10.

Nathan, Dev, Govind Kelkar, Pierre Walter (2004), *Globalization and Indigenous People in Asia: Changing the Local-Global Interface.* New Delhi: Sage Publications.

Sarin, Madhu (1995), 'Regenerating India's Forests: Reconciling Gender Equity with Joint Forest Management'. *IDA Bulletin* 26 (1): 83-91.

Sathyanarayanan, C.R. (2003), Sharing and Collective Existence: Tenets of Livelihood Pursuits among the Muduvans of Anamalai Hills, South India. *http//www.sasnet.lu.se.*

Siva Vandana (1989), *Staying Alive: Women, Ecology and Development.* London: Zed Books.

Sury, M.M. (2001), *India: A Decade of Economic Reforms* 1991-2001. New Delhi: New Century Publications.

Thurston, Edgar. (1909), *Castes and Tribes of Southern India* Vol. 11. New Delhi: Cosmo Publications.

Mini P.V.

Economic Reforms and Deprivations of An Artisan Tribe-Kerala Experience

12

INTRODUCTION

Society comprises a group of people, whose lives are interrelated to each other in someway or the other. There can be different societies and the concept of society is flexible. One society can exist within another or overlap it. The economy of a society links with the existence of people, agricultural fields, forests, factories, consumable goods etc. Natural, cultural and human resources are utilized to fill our economic wants. The tribal economy is a mixed one and household industries and crafts occupy a prominent position among the subsidiary occupations. Majumdar and Madan classify the tribes on the basis of their economic pattern and occupation[1].

The development of any economy largely depends upon the reforms adopted by the administrators. Economic reforms are to achieve rapid economic development to improve the living standards of the people and to eliminate poverty in terms of basic social amenities such as safe drinking water, sanitation facilities and primary education, but the achievements were far from satisfactory. With the implementation of the Structural Adjustment Reforms, at the national level, some changes have occurred in the Kerala's economy during the decade of the 1990's. Kerala's unemployment, both urban and rural, has been growing and reached an alarming level by the beginning of the millennium.

Tribal communities of Kerala has been classified[2] into six groups based on their subsistence pattern. viz., Hunters-Gatherers and Forest dwellers, Shifting cultivators or Punam cultivators, Artisans & Craft workers, Marginal farmers and agricultural laborers, Settled Agriculturists, Bonded Labourers and Estate workers. At the same time they follow subsidiary occupations such as craft works. Forest regulations and land alienation have changed the subsistent activities of these communities. Therefore, most of the members of these communities forced to give up their traditional economic activities, such as, artisan works and shifting cultivations, and there by become agricultural labourers. Tribal artisans combined their crafts with food gathering, hunting or shifting cultivation. These artisans made agricultural implements, pots, baskets, etc., for those who had taken to settled agriculture and in return accepted food grains from them, for their continued activities. Their role can be properly appreciated only in relation to the needs of other groups, regionally.

GEOGRAPHY & TRIBAL COMMUNITIES OF WYNAD

Wynad situated 90 kms North east of Calicut City of Malabar in Northern Kerala, has about half of the tribal population of the State. Formerly, Wynad was a part of Nilgiri plateau. The extreme eastern half of Wynad, contiguous with the Nilgiris and Coorg, is inhabited by the Kanarese speaking tribes and the western half by the Malayalam speaking tribes. These hilly regions formed a part of the territory of the Pazhassi Raja during the British regime. 35.82% of the total tribal population of the State lives in Wayanad. According to 2001 census, (see Table 1) the tribal population of Wynad is 136, 062 (67,394 males and 68,668 females). Adiyan, Paniyan, Kattunaicken alias Thenkuruman or Jenukuruman, Vettakuruman alias Uralikuruman, Mullukuruman and Kurichyans are the major tribal folks of Wynad. Small tribal communities like Karimpalan, Thachanadan Moopan and Wyandan Kadars are also seen in this District. (see Table 2). Of them Vettakurumans alias Uralikurumans are considered as the Artisan tribes of Wynad. They are inhibiting in Northern and Central parts of Wynad such as Thirunelli, Begur, Tholpetty, Panamaram, Poothadi, Noolpuzha, Kaniyampatta, Pulpally, Mullankolli and Kurichyad forests.

Table 1
Scheduled Caste and Scheduled Tribe Population–2001 Census

Sl. No.	*District*	*Scheduled Caste*			*Scheduled Tribe*			*Scheduled Tribe*
		Total	*Male*	*Female*	*Total*	*Male*	*Female*	*Percentage*
1.	Thiruvananthapuram	370,857	178,718	192,139	20,893	9,890	11,003	0.65
2.	Kollam	322,887	156,880	166,007	5,190	2,447	2,743	0.20
3.	Pathanamthitta	162,002	78,731	83,271	6,549	3,184	3,365	0.53
4.	Alappuzha	199,231	96,900	102,331	3,131	1,565	1,566	0.15
5.	Kottayam	150,282	73,885	76,397	18,340	8,972	9,368	0.94
6.	Idukki	159,362	79,389	79,973	50,973	25,510	25,463	4.51
7.	Ernakulam	263,518	129,706	133,812	10,046	5,079	4,967	0.32
8.	Thrissur	354,226	171,443	182,783	4,826	2,293	2,533	0.16
9.	Palakkad	432,578	210,624	221,954	39,665	19,990	19,675	1.52
10.	Malappuram	285,442	140,535	144,907	12,267	5,996	6,271	0.34
11.	Kozhikode	200,983	98,386	102,597	5,940	2,924	3,016	0.21
12.	Wayanad	33,364	16,738	16,626	13,60,62	67,394	68,668	17.43
13.	Kannur	98,991	48,275	50,716	19,969	9,793	10,176	0.83
14.	Kasargode	90,218	44,904	45,314	30,338	15,132	15,206	2.52
	G. Total	3,123,941	1,525,114	1,598,827	364,189	180,169	184,020	1.14

Source: Scheduled Tribe Development Department, Thiruvananthapuram.

Table 2
Tribal folk of Wynad & their Occupation

Sl. No.	*Name of the Tribe*	*Occupation*
1.	Adiyan	Agricultural labourers
2.	Kattunayakan (Jenukuruman/Thenkuruman)	Hunters-gatherers/casual labours
3.	Kurichiyain	Settled cultivators
4.	Karimpalan	Agricultural labourers & Marginal farmers
5.	Mullukuruman	Settled cultivators
6.	Paniyan	Agricultural labourers
7.	Thachanadan Mooppan	Agricultural labourers & Marginal farmers
8.	Vettakuruman (Uralikuruman)	Artisans/casual labourers
9.	Wynad Kadar	Agricultural labourers & Marginal farmers

The major crops of the Wynad district are of coconut, areacanut, rubber, pepper, banana, cashew, rice and vegetables. There are also extensive tea and coffee plantations. Species like ginger, cardamom and turmeric are also cultivated in the district to a large extent.

Tribal people in general derived a substantial amount of their livelihood, either directly or indirectly, from the forests. They build their houses by means of locally available raw materials like timber, bamboo and grass, which are collected from nearby forests. Even for the purpose of binding or fixing the poles in the constructions, creepers of bark are used rather than iron nails. Thus, present paper seeks to explore the issues related to the traditional artisan skills of Vettakurumans, the problems encountered by them while adapting to the present scenario by looking into the economic reforms and deprivations of these artisans.

ARTISAN WORKS OF VETTAKURUMANS

The existing structure of the tribal crafts brings it close to the household industry, a new word brought into the economic realm by the Census of India, 1961. The household industry is defined "as *an industry managed by the head of the household himself or mainly by members of the household at home or within the rural areas ad only at home in urban areas*". Such an industry is relatively small and can relate itself to production, processing, servicing, repairing, making and selling of goods. Thus, tribal crafts fall under household industries. (Sao; 1988). Tribal crafts entirely different from that of village industries or small scale industries. The artisan skill is mostly community oriented and the skills, therefore, remain confined to a particular tribal community due to the process of inheritance. (Basu and Bhattacharya, 1987). According to C. Gopalan Nair (1911) "*These men are artisans and are handy at all kinds of work. They make ploughs and knives as any blacksmith does, earthen pots that last longer than those made by professional potters, cut and size timber just as any carpenter, make umbrellas of screw pine leaves, are skilled in basket work and gather honey from the tallest tree*".

For carpentry work Vettakurumans use hardwood found in nearby forest areas for making various house hold articles. Articles like wooden stool, table, door panels and frames, agricultural implements, wooden harrow and wooden yok are generally manufactured by this tribe. They are engaged in various types of black smithy works like, the preparation, repairing, sharpening and mending of various types of tools and implements such as sickle, axe, spade iron head of arrow, long plough share, bows and arrows for hunting purposes used by the other tribes of Wayanad. Vettakurumans also practice hand made pottery. They developed a skill in making basket with special patterns based on local traditions and equipments. They weave beautiful baskets (*kutta*) from a kind of grass, called as *Manipullu.* These baskets are used for storing agricultural produces such as cereals. They collect this type of grass from the paddy fields and riversides, whenever there is scarcity, it will be brought from Kodaku. Tender grasses are used for weaving purposes because it gives strength than older grass. Both men and women are making mats (panambu), made up of bamboo poles.

PROBLEMS OF TRIBAL ARTISANS

Almost all the forest areas are protected or declared as reserve forests. Tribes have hardly any access to dense forest area for collecting the raw materials. Hence procuring of raw materials is a big problem for the tribal artisans. (Nageswar Rao, 1991). Tribal economy is characterized by dependence on forest as an ecological niche, a resource of living and food supply. Non tribes, migrated into tribal regions and carried with them the superior technology of agricultural cultivation, use of implements, and concept of agriculture seasons, which were accepted by some sections of the tribals living in the valleys. The insufficient supply of raw materials posses a serious problems for some tribal artisans. Today pot making ceased because they fail to get suitable clay for making it. Now with the popularity of aluminum and steel vessels their traditional hand made skill have become obsolete. Scarcity of grass is another factor for making baskets. The high price of raw materials causes low production in black smithy and thus creates high idle capacity in the sector. Even if the raw materials are available to them, the artisans sit idly for days together because they do not possess the appropriate implements fort manufacturing. They are efficient carpenters and are capable of producing even non traditional items, if required tools made available to them.

At present these craftsmen are unable to sell their products for a reasonable price. Lack of bargaining power compels them to sell goods even below the cost of production. Today these people are facing great difficulty to find out a proper market for their products, and also in snatching away of their craft work opportunities by artisans coming up from non-tribals.Under this circumstances they are unable to compete with the non-tribals. Now they themselves are struggling to make both ends meet. Their craft forms require support for protection, revitalization and encouragement.

'The switching over of tribal artisans from their original craft activity to some other activities like agriculture and wage earning leads to deterioration of skill' (Chakrabarty, 1980). Thus retaining those craftsmen, who inherit the working skill, but want to leave the sector due to low productivity and low returns posses a major problem. Hand made pottery was also done rarely today as the youth preferred plantation and paddy field works under non tribal landlords for an earning without much discomfort, while they earned very little from their handmade potteries in the past. Nowadays, they could not continue their traditional manufacturing of baskets and mats as the forest Department did not allow them to enter into forests for chopping off bamboo and reeds.

TRIBAL ECONOMY IN THE CHANGING SCENARIO

Earlier barter economy[3] was mostly prevalent among tribal communities. The articles of domestic use are sold to the settlers in exchange of money. Pressure falls on tribal artisans when demand of products comes down, forcing them to offer cheap rates to the traders.

The transformation of the tribal economy from a barter system to cash economy and this type of market based economy occurred in a very short span of time. Today their economy demands successful entrepreneurs. Even though, certain raining programmes were conducted to improve their efficiency in pottery and blacksmithy they failed to produce the expected result. For instance, a few years back a training programme in wheel made pottery was given to a few tribal youths of Vettakurumans. The purpose of the training programme has not served as there has been no follow up action from the organizers. As a result they still sit idle for want of investment capitals and non availability of raw materials. The absence of organizers to look after the supply of raw materials and sale of the finished goods is responsible for this situation. Therefore a solution can be brought out only by promoting entrepreneurship among the tribal artisans. If they received training in modern techniques along with their traditional skill it will help them to adapt themselves to the present day scenario. This, in turn will empower them to compete with the mainstream society.

CONCLUSION

It is important to emphasize that reforms should not focus only on the rich and ignore the rest. The essence of reform is to increase the productivity of all sections of society by making competition-free and access to markets easier. Government and other related NGO's have a major role to play in ensuring that the growth process is indeed broad based, so that the benefits are widespread. Vettakurumans possess a variety of traditional skills to earn their livelihood. Even though the art forms created by them are rich in artistic skill and originality, they are not in a position to market their craft forms. So Government should provide facilities for marketing their goods and offer training in modern techniques of craft works. Thus, the traditional skills of Vettakurumans can be preserved for prosperity according to the changing scenario.

NOTES

1. 1. food gathering (hunting and fishing) 2. Agriculture. 3. Shifting cultivation 4. Handicraft. 5. Pastoralism. 6. Industrial labour.
2. This classification is on the basis of the subsistence pattern of these communities in the recent past.
3. Artisans exchange their products of domestic use for food products, items of day to day use and even clothes.